Instant Pot for Two Cookbook

Delicious, Simple and Quick Instant Pot Recipes for Two

Table of Contents

INTRODUCTION

Welcome!

If you're reading this then I assume you are the owner of an Instant Pot, and you are one half of a hungry pair. Whether you're cooking for yourself and a spouse or partner, or for a friend or roommate, you've landed at the right spot! There are many cookbooks out there for large families, but what about families of two? Never fear, in this book you will find lots of recipes, which are ideal for 2 people (with leftovers, of course!).

Cooking for 2 people doesn't need to be too different to cooking for 5 or 6. In fact, you don't need to change much apart from the quantities. However, I can completely sympathize with the dilemma of "is it worth cooking this just for the two of us?". I've often considered making a fancy meal for my partner and I, only to give up and opt for eggs on toast. The great thing about the Instant Pot is that it takes away a lot of the effort and hard work of cooking, so you can create a beautiful meal for two without exerting yourself!

THE INSTANT POT

What is the Instant Pot?

The Instant Pot is a genius creation, made to make the lives of couples and small families easier. In more specific terms, it's an electric pressure cooker with many different functions and cooking options. The Instant Pot shape shifts into a rice cooker, slow cooker, warmer, soup maker, stew maker, and steamer. Some models even have a yoghurt-making function!

Benefits: why use it?

Tidy and cost-effective

Pots, pans, and kitchen appliances are expensive, so if you want to avoid having to spend-up large on kitchen supplies, then owning an Instant Pot is a very smart option. Your cupboards, draws, and benches can remain uncluttered as your Instant Pot doubles as many different appliances and equipment (steamer, rice cooker, saucepan, slow cooker).

Easy

With the Instant Pot, it's really as simple as pressing a few buttons. You don't need to study a complicated recipe and follow strict instructions to create an amazing meal as the Instant Pot does it for you! This is ideal for couples who aren't home chefs, but still want to enjoy quality meals.

Quick

The high pressure and temperature of pressure cooking cuts regular cooking times down by a large degree. If you want dinner on the table ASAP, then the Instant Pot is your best friend. Dishes such as roasts and large portions of meat which usually take a long time to cook can be ready in under an hour.

Versatile

You can play around with lots of different dishes throughout the week with the Instant Pot, thanks to the many different cooking methods provided. Steamed veggies and fish, fried burger patties, rich stews, creamy soups, slow-cooked meat... the possibilities are vast.

Safe cooking, sanitary food

Kitchen safety is very important, and you can rest assured that The Instant Pot will keep you safe while cooking, and your food safe to eat. The high pressure and temperature kills even the tiniest of bacteria, making your food sanitary and safe. The pot has been designed for safety when it comes to pressure – the lid will never fly off and explode everywhere! You have total control over the pot; you can leave it to release the pressure on its own, or you can safely release the pressure yourself.

How to use it

Brown your meat

If you're cooking a meat-based dish, you can use the Sauté function first to brown and seal the meat before pressure cooking. This locks moisture and flavor into the meat.

Simmer your booze

If you're using alcohol in your dish, such as wine or dark liquor, you can use the Sauté function to simmer the alcohol away before you pressure cook the dish. This means that the strong alcohol flavor evaporates, leaving a rich and lovely undertone of the wine or liquor. The same goes for sauces and jus, you can simmer them using the Sauté function until thick and glossy.

Note: always leave the lid OFF when using the Sauté function.

Load it up

Now you can load the pot with your ingredients. Don't fill the pot further than 2/3 full for the best results.

Give it a drink

The Instant Pot needs liquid in order to function properly. Use at least 8floz of liquid, whether it's stock, water, tinned tomatoes, wine, or fruit juice.

Select the function and secure the lid

Now you can twist the lid onto the pot and listen out for the beep which tells you the lid is secure. Press the button which best suits your dish, i.e. for soup, press the SOUP button, for rice, press the RICE button, or simply use the MANUAL button if you're unsure. You can adjust the pressure from HIGH to LOW with the manual button.

Adjust the time

Use the plus and minus symbols to adjust the time according to your recipe (or your amazing chef-like instincts!). The pot will now begin to build pressure and temperature, and once it does, it will begin to cook for the amount of time you have specified.

Note: ensure the steam valve is on "seal" for all functions except SLOW COOK when it must always be set to "vent".

Release the pressure

When the pot has finished cooking, it will sing out to you with a beep. You can either leave it alone to release the pressure by itself, or you can carefully flick the steam valve from "sealed" to "vent" using a tea towel wrapped around your hand, and keeping your face and body clear of the steam valve.

Why it's perfect for two

Perfect fit

All Instant Pot models are a perfect size for two people, as you can create a meal plus leftovers/lunch for two. Kill two birds with one stone every night and get your dinner and lunch sorted in one handy pot.

No-fights cooking

If you've ever had an argument with a live-in friend or partner about who's cooking dinner tonight, then the Instant pot might just save your relationship. It's so easy to create a wonderful meal with the Instant Pot there's really nothing to fight about! You could be on dinner duty every night and never feel like you're being overworked in the domestic department. Throw the ingredients in, press the button, count down the minutes, eat.

No-fights clean up

When you create a meal with your Instant Pot, the only dish you need to clean is the inner pot, and this is easy! Throw it in the dishwasher or simply rinse it out, dry it, and place it back into the Instant Pot. No more fighting over who's doing the dishes! See? The Instant Pot is a peace maker as well as a versatile cooker.

Discreet and compact for small kitchens

If you and your partner or friend live in a small apartment or unit, chances are you have a small kitchen with little bench and storage space. The Instant Pot can sit neatly on your bench and act as your main cooking station for all kinds of dishes, eliminating the need for other bulky appliances and equipment to clog up your kitchen.

INSTANT POT RECIPES

About these recipes

Servings

Of course, these recipes make enough for two people, because that's the name of the game! However, many of these recipes make enough for 2 people, plus leftovers for the next day (or late at night, straight from the fridge after binge watching Netflix? No? Just me. Okay. Moving on). Like always, you can adjust the quantities of the ingredients to make more or less food.

Time

Each recipe has an approximate time provide at the start. It's important to note that these approximate times do NOT include the time the Instant Pot takes to reach heat and pressure. The time provided only takes into account the preparation of the dish and the actual cooking time. Also, you may be quicker or slower cook than me, so you might find that your preparation time is more or less than the recipe states.

Methods and Instant Pot settings

I hope you don't mind that many of these recipes only utilize the SAUTE function on your Instant Pot. This is because many of these recipes only require a bit of frying or sautéing. However, there are many opportunities to use the other functions too!

Quick release

For the majority of these recipes I have suggested you quick-release the pressure straight after cooking, because I want these recipes to be quick and easy for you. However, if you want to naturally release the pressure, then go ahead! You might just want to lower the cooking time slightly to make up for the extra time in the pot. Foods such as fish and vegetables can be overcooked easily so just take note of cooking times and adjust accordingly.

Salt, pepper and olive oil

Just a quick note here regarding salt, pepper and olive oil. I haven't added these three ingredients to the ingredients lists because I assume you have these ingredients in your larder. When it says to "drizzle" some olive oil into the Instant Pot, this means a rough tablespoon. A "pinch" or "sprinkling" of salt and pepper just means a little scattering to suit your taste. Everyone's salt and pepper preferences are different, so use as much or as little as you wish.

Garlic

A very quick note: I LOVE garlic, so I have added lots of garlic to these recipes. If you come across a recipe calling for four garlic cloves when you would usually use one, then by all means, use as many or as few as you'd like!

Meat

Meat-loving pairs pay attention! This section is full of delicious, meaty recipes for steak, lamb, and pork. You will find treasures such as roasts, burgers, skewers...and many more.

Steaks with Garlic Cream Sauce

Steak is a far more affordable meal when it's just for two! I like eye fillet steaks, but you can use any cut you like best. The garlic cream sauce is rich, silky, and very luxurious. Serve with freshly-steamed green beans for a hit of freshness.

Time: approximately 25 minutes

Ingredients:
- Olive oil
- 2 steaks, room temperature
- Salt and pepper, to taste
- 4 garlic cloves, finely chopped
- ½ tsp fresh oregano, finely chopped
- ¼ cup dry white wine
- ¾ cup heavy cream

Method:
1. Press the SAUTE button on your Instant Pot and adjust the temperature to HIGH, drizzle some olive oil into the pot.
2. Once the oil is very hot, carefully place the steaks into the pot and cook according to your preference (rare, medium, well done), turn the steak and cook the other side.
3. Remove the steaks from the pot and leave on a board to rest, and sprinkle the steaks with salt and pepper at this stage.
4. Don't wash the Instant Pot before you make the sauce, the leftover steak juices will add lovely flavor to the sauce.
5. Keep the Instant Pot on the SAUTE function, but adjust the temperature to NORMAL.
6. Add the garlic, herbs, and wine to the pot, sauté until the wine has reduced and the smell of alcohol has disappeared.
7. Add the cream, salt, and pepper to the pot and stir to combine.
8. Simmer the sauce for about 5 minutes until thick and creamy.
9. Serve the steak with a generous helping of creamy garlic sauce spooned over the top.

Lamb Skewers with Pita Bread and Eggplant Dip

One of the best ways to enjoy lamb for a light and simple meal is to place tender cubes of lamb steak onto skewers, and serve with a warm pita bread. This recipe turns the volume up by adding a delicious eggplant pita filling!

Time: approximately 30 minutes

Ingredients:
- Olive oil
- 2 lamb steaks, cut into cubes
- Salt and pepper
- ½ tsp ground cumin
- ½ tsp chili powder
- 3 garlic cloves, finely chopped
- 1 large eggplant, cut into chunks
- ½ cup plain Greek yogurt
- 2 pita breads (store bought is fine)

Method:
1. Press the SAUTE button on your Instant Pot and adjust the temperature to HIGH, drizzle some olive oil into the pot.
2. Coat the lamb with salt, pepper, cumin, and chili powder.
3. Once the oil is very hot, add the lamb cubes and sauté for about 5 minutes, turning a few times so the lamb cubes are golden and brown on all sides.
4. Take the lamb cubes out of the pot and leave aside, don't wash the pot (the lamb juices and leftover spices will flavor the eggplant!).
5. Keep the Instant Pot on the sauté function, adjust the temperature to NORMAL.
6. Drizzle some more olive oil into the Instant Pot and add the garlic, cook for about 20 seconds until the garlic is soft.
7. Add the eggplant and keep stirring as the eggplant sautés and becomes soft and mushy.
8. Remove the eggplant and place into a small bowl, add the yogurt, salt, and pepper, stir to combine.
9. Toast the pita breads and fill with eggplant filling, lamb cubes, and any other fillings you desire (baby spinach is a great match!).

Mini Pork Roast

Don't let the fact that you're only feeding 2 people put you off making a delicious roast dinner. A small pork loin is more than enough to feed 2 people for a meal, plus leftovers. Serve with roasted potatoes and peas.

Time: approximately 40 minutes

Ingredients:
- ½ cup (4fl oz) apple juice
- 1 cup (8fl oz) stock (veggie or chicken)
- 1 apple, cut into 5 pieces
- Small pork loin (approximately 1 lb), sprinkled with salt and pepper
- Olive oil

Method:
1. Pour the apple juice and stock into the Instant Pot.
2. Place the apple chunks and pork loin into the pot (it will sit in the liquid).
3. Secure the lid onto the pot and press the MEAT/STEW button, adjust the time to 20 minutes.
4. Once the pot beeps, quick-release the pressure and remove the lid.
5. Place the pork loin onto a board to rest as you heat a skillet or fry pan with a drizzle of oil.
6. Once the fry pan is very hot, place the cooked pork loin into the pan and fry on all sides for a minute or so, or until crispy and golden.
7. You can utilize the leftover liquid in the Instant Pot by pressing the SAUTE button and simmering the liquid until reduced (on NORMAL heat).
8. Serve with your favorite vegetables and a drizzle of reduced liquid.
9. Any leftover meat will make an amazing sandwich!

Lamb Steaks with Feta and Potatoes

Lamb steaks make for a refreshing change from beef steaks. Feta cheese and sautéed potatoes accompany the sweet, tender meat for an easy and yummy dinner for two.

Time: approximately 30 minutes

Ingredients:
- 2 medium-large potatoes, skin on, cut into cubes
- Salt and pepper, to taste
- Olive oil
- 2 lamb steaks
- ½ tsp dried mixed herbs
- 3 garlic cloves, sliced
- 5 oz feta cheese, crumbled

Method:
1. Pour 2 cups of water into the Instant Pot and place the steaming basket into the pot.
2. Place the potato cubes into the steaming basket and sprinkle with salt.
3. Secure the lid onto the pot and press the STEAM button, adjust the time to 3 minutes.
4. Once the pot beeps, quick-release the pressure and remove the lid.
5. Take the basket of potatoes out of the pot and set aside, discard any leftover water from the pot.
6. Drizzle some olive oil into the Instant Pot and press the SAUTE button, adjust the temperature to HIGH.
7. Sprinkle the lamb with salt, pepper, and herbs, and once the oil is hot, add the steaks to the pot and cook for about 1 minute each side, (or more if you prefer more well-done meat).
8. Remove the lamb steaks from the pot and place on a board to rest. Don't wash the pot, just leave it as it is.
9. Place the garlic into the pot and adjust the temperature to NORMAL (the pot should still be on the SAUTE function), sauté the garlic for about 30 seconds.
10. Add the steamed potatoes to the pot and stir to coat in oil and garlic, sauté for about 5 minutes until crispy and golden, don't worry if they get a bit mushy, that's part of the charm!
11. Before serving, stir the feta cheese into the potatoes.

Cold Beef Noodle Salad

For a refreshing Summertime dinner for two, this cold beef noodle salad really does the trick. You could even double the recipe so you've both got a ready-made lunch for the next day!

Time: approximately 20 minutes

Ingredients:
- 10 oz dried rice noodles (flat or vermicelli, any kind works)
- Olive oil
- 1 large sirloin steak (about 1 lb)
- Salt and pepper, to taste
- 1 scallion, finely chopped
- Handful of fresh coriander, finely chopped
- 1 fresh red chili, finely chopped (seeds removed if you don't want too much spice)
- 1 fresh lime
- 1 tsp brown sugar
- 1 tsp sesame oil (if you have it)
- 2 tsp fish sauce (if you have it, you can use soy sauce as a substitute)

Method:
1. Bring a pot of water to the boil and add the rice noodles, cook until soft (or follow the packet instructions if they need alternate cooking methods, some are pre-cooked and just need to be soaked in hot water), run cold water over the noodles until they are cold, then leave aside.
2. Press the SAUTE button on your Instant Pot and adjust the temperature to HIGH, drizzle some olive oil into the pot.
3. Once the oil is hot, add the steak to the pot and cook for about 2 minutes on both sides, or longer if you want your steak well done.
4. Remove the steak from the pot and place on a board to rest, sprinkle with salt and pepper.
5. In a large salad bowl, add the scallions, coriander, chili, juice of one lime, brown sugar, sesame oil, and fish or soy sauce, stir to combine.
6. Add the cooked noodles and toss to coat in the dressing.
7. Slice the steak into thin strips and scatter over the noodle salad before serving.

Pulled Pork Burgers

On a lazy Friday night, you and your loved one should absolutely make these amazing pulled pork burgers. If you want to make it a full-on meal, add some oven-baked, home-cut fries and a fresh coleslaw!

Time: approximately 55 minutes

Ingredients:
- ½ tsp ground cumin
- ½ tsp ground coriander
- ½ tsp paprika
- 2 tbsp tomato ketchup
- 1 tsp Worcester sauce (or soy sauce as a substitute)
- 1 tbsp brown sugar
- 1 cup (8fl oz) apple juice
- Salt and pepper, to taste
- 1 lb pork shoulder
- 1 onion, roughly chopped
- 2 brioche buns
- 2 tbsp mayonnaise (1tbsp per burger)
- 2 slices of cheddar cheese (or any other cheese)
- 1 apple, grated

Method:
1. Place the onion, cumin, coriander, paprika, ketchup, Worcester or soy sauce, brown sugar, apple juice, salt, and pepper into the Instant Pot, stir to combine.
2. Place the pork shoulder and onion into the pot.
3. Secure the lid onto the pot and press the MEAT/STEW button, adjust the time to 45 minutes.
4. Once the pot beeps, quick-release the pressure and remove the lid.
5. Place the pork onto a board to rest while you heat a skillet or fry pan.
6. Once the pan is hot, place the pork skin-side down onto the pan and fry until golden and crispy.
7. Simmer the leftover liquid in the Instant Pot on the SAUTE function until reduced and thick.
8. With 2 forks, shred the pork meat into pieces.

9. Grill the brioche buns under the grill in the oven, or place them cut-side down on a hot, oiled skillet.

10. Spread the buns with mayonnaise, then place a generous pile of pulled pork on top, then a sprinkle of grated apple, then the cheese (you could also grill the cheese onto the bun if you want it to be extra melted).

11. Drizzle some of the reduced liquid from the Instant Pot over onto the burger before serving!

Easy Pork Stir Fry

Whenever I need a quick and nutritious dinner with a good mix of meat and veggies, my first thought is always "stir fry!" This one uses pork, broccoli, carrots, and red capsicum. There are no rules... use any veggies you like if you don't fancy these ones!

Time: approximately 20 minutes

Ingredients:
- Olive oil
- 1 lb pork steak, cut into cubes
- ½ head of broccoli, cut into florets
- 2 carrots, peeled and cut into even chunks
- 1 red capsicum, seeds and core removed, cut into slices
- 3 garlic cloves, finely chopped
- 1 tbsp grated fresh garlic
- 3tbsp soy sauce
- 1 tbsp fish sauce
- 1 tsp brown sugar
- 1/3 cup roasted, salted cashew nuts

Method:
1. Press the SAUTE button on your Instant Pot, adjust the temperature to HIGH, and drizzle some olive oil into the pot.
2. Add the pork cubes to the pot and sauté for about 3 minutes until golden.
3. Add the broccoli, carrots, capsicum, and garlic, sauté for a further 2 minutes until the veggies are just starting to cook through (I like my stir-fried veggies to be crispy, but you can cook yours for longer if you'd like them to be softer).
4. Add the soy sauce, fish sauce, brown sugar, and pepper to the pot and stir to coat the pork and veggies.
5. Serve immediately, with a sprinkling of cashew nuts.
6. If you're extra hungry you could serve with a pile of fluffy rice.

INSTANT POT FOR TWO COOKBOOK

Rack of Lamb with Herb Butter

If you're on cooking duty and you want to make something impressive for the other half of your pair, then lamb racks are the way to go! Herb butter adds a touch of decadence and class.

Time: approximately 35 minutes

Ingredients:
- Olive oil
- Enough lamb racks for two (about 1lb)
- ¾ cup red wine
- 4 garlic cloves, finely chopped
- 1 sprig fresh rosemary
- Salt and pepper, to taste
- 2 tbsp butter
- ½ tsp dried mixed herbs
- ½ sea salt

Method:
1. Press the SAUTE button on your Instant Pot and adjust the temperature to HIGH, drizzle some olive oil into the pot.
2. Once the oil is hot, add the lamb racks to the pot and sauté for about 2 minutes until golden and sealed.
3. Press the MEAT/STEW button and adjust the time to 20 minutes.
4. Add the red wine, garlic, rosemary, salt, and pepper to the pot.
5. Secure the lid onto the pot.
6. Once the pot beeps, quick-release the pressure and remove the lid.
7. Remove the lamb racks from the pot and set aside to rest.
8. Press the SAUTE button and adjust the time to NORMAL.
9. Simmer the remaining liquid in the pot until reduced and thickened.
10. To make the butter, simply mix together the butter, dried herbs, and sea salt.
11. Serve the lamb racks with a drizzle of the reduced liquid, herb butter, and any veggies of your choice.

Lamb Stew for Two

Cheaper cuts of lamb are made for stew. This stew has onions, parsnips, and sweet potatoes to add bulk and nutrition. This makes a perfect Winter lunch as well, so double the recipe and get your Tupperware ready!

Time: approximately 55 minutes

Ingredients:
- 1 lb stewing lamb, cut into cubes and tossed in 2tbsp plain flour
- 1 large onion, roughly chopped
- 5 garlic cloves, finely chopped
- 1 large parsnip, peeled and chopped into chunks
- 2 carrots, peeled and chopped into chunks
- 1 cup (8fl oz) red wine
- 1.5 cups (12fl oz) lamb stock
- ½ tsp dried rosemary
- Salt and pepper, to taste

Method:
1. Press the SAUTE button on your Instant Pot and adjust the temperature to NORMAL.
2. Add the flour-coated lamb to the pot and sauté for a few minutes until browned.
3. Add the onions and garlic, sauté for about 30 seconds to soften slightly.
4. Add the parsnip, carrots, wine, stock, rosemary, salt, and pepper.
5. Secure the lid onto the pot and press the MEAT/STEW button, adjust the time to 45 minutes.
6. Once the pot beeps, quick-release the pressure and remove the lid.
7. Stir the stew before serving with veggies and a glass of red wine!

Potato-top Beef, Mushroom, and Bacon Pie

If you ever go to Australia or New Zealand you'll be sure to come across the long-standing culinary trend of eating meat pies from the service station or bakery. One of the best varieties is the potato-top pie. This one has mushrooms and bacon as well...just to make it even more delicious. Serve with ketchup and some greens (so you don't feel guilty!). If you don't have a pie dish suitable for two people, then you could use two single pie dishes instead.

Time: approximately 1 hour

Ingredients:
- Olive oil
- 1 onion, finely chopped
- 1 lb minced beef
- 3 rashers of streaky bacon, cut into small pieces
- 1 large Portobello mushroom, thinly sliced
- 1 cup (8fl oz) beef stock
- Salt and pepper, to taste
- 1 tbsp butter
- Store-bought puff pastry
- 3 medium-sized potatoes, peeled and cut into chunks

Method:
1. Preheat the oven to 390 degrees Fahrenheit.
2. Press the SAUTE button on your Instant Pot and keep the temperature at NORMAL, drizzle some olive oil into the pot.
3. Add the onions and beef to the pot and sauté until the beef has browned and the onions are soft.
4. Add the bacon and mushrooms to the pot and sauté until the mushrooms soften and the bacon begins to sizzle and cook (about 3 minutes).
5. Add the beef stock, salt, and pepper to the pot, stir to combine.
6. Simmer the beef mixture until thick and rich (about 10 minutes).
7. While the beef mixture simmers, prepare the pie dish or dishes by greasing them with butter and lining them with pastry.
8. To prepare the potatoes, boil them in a pot of water (enough water to just cover the potatoes) until they are soft. Use a potato masher or fork to mash the potatoes until soft, stir through the butter, salt, and pepper.

9. Fill the pie(s) with the beef mixture and then spoon the mashed potato on top, you can use a piping bag to make a neat and fancy pattern, but rustic is just as good!

10. Place the pie(s) into the preheated oven and bake for about 25 minutes, the potato will be golden and the pastry should be flaky and golden when you turn the pies out onto a dish before eating.

Spicy Lamb Chops and Root Veggie Mash

Lamb chops are yummy enough as they are, but they become extra special when you add a touch of spice. As for the mash...well, you could make plain mashed potatoes, but why not make something even yummier and add parsnips and carrots?

Time: approximately 45 minutes

Ingredients:
- 4 lamb chops (2 per serving, add more if you'd like larger portions)
- 1 tsp chili powder
- ½ tsp paprika
- 4 garlic cloves, crushed
- Salt and pepper, to taste
- 1 cup (8fl oz) lamb stock
- 1 large potato, peeled and chopped into cubes
- 2 carrots, peeled and chopped into chunks
- 1 large parsnip, peeled and chopped into chunks
- 1 knob of butter

Method:
1. Rub the lamb chops with chili powder, paprika, garlic, salt, and pepper.
2. Place the lamb chops, stock, potato, carrots, and parsnip into the pot.
3. Secure the lid onto the pot and press the MEAT/STEW button, adjust the time to 7 minutes (or cook on manual pressure on high).
4. Once the pot beeps, quick-release the pressure and remove the lid.
5. Take the chops out and place on a board to rest.
6. With a potato masher, mash the remaining veggies and liquid in the pot until a smooth mash forms.
7. Stir the knob of butter through the mash until melted.
8. Serve the lamb chops on top of a pile of buttery mash!

Creamy Beef Curry for Two

Beef goes very well with warming, spicy flavors and creamy sauce. This curry is mild and comforting, and it's even better when served with rice and naan bread. Resist the urge to get takeout on a Friday night and make this curry instead, I promise it's just as satisfying!

Time: approximately 30 minutes

Ingredients:
- Olive oil
- 1 onion, finely chopped
- 3 garlic cloves, finely chopped
- 1 tbsp grated fresh ginger
- 2 tbsp red curry paste (any good supermarket or Asian store will supply high-quality curry pastes)
- 14 oz stewing beef, cubed
- 1 ½ cups (12fl oz) full-fat coconut cream
- 1 ½ cups (12fl oz) beef stock
- Salt and pepper, to taste

Method:
1. Drizzle some olive oil into the Instant Pot and press the SAUTE button, keep the temperature at NORMAL.
2. Add the onion, garlic, ginger, and curry paste, sauté until fragrant (about 2 minutes).
3. Add the beef to the pot and stir to coat in curry paste, sauté for a couple of minutes to seal the beef.
4. Add the coconut cream, beef stock, salt, and pepper to the pot and stir to combine.
5. Secure the lid onto the pot and press the MEAT/STEW button, adjust the time to 20 minutes.
6. Once the pot beeps, quick-release the pressure and remove the lid.
7. Serve the curry with hot basmati rice and a warm, buttered naan bread

Low-carb Beef and Beetroot Burgers

This is for all the couples out there who are trying to get fit and healthy despite the temptations of carbs, sweet treats, and takeout! You can still have an amazing burger without adding extra carbs. This burger is cased within lettuce leaves, and filled with beef, beetroot, pickles, mustard, and a little sliver of cheese.

Time: approximately 25 minutes

Ingredients
- 1 lb minced beef
- 1 egg
- ½ cup breadcrumbs
- 1 tsp dried mixed herbs
- Salt and pepper, to taste
- Olive oil
- 2 medium-sized iceberg lettuce leaves per burger (so 4 leaves for 2 burgers etc.)
- 1 tsp per burger of Dijon mustard
- 1 tsp per burger of mayonnaise
- Sharp cheddar cheese, small slice per burger
- 1 small tin of sliced beetroot
- Bread and butter pickles, sliced (or your favorite type of pickles)

Method:
1. In a medium-sized bowl, combine the minced beef, egg, breadcrumbs, dried mixed herbs, salt, and pepper.
2. Press the SAUTE button on your Instant Pot and keep the temperature at NORMAL, drizzle some olive oil into the pot.
3. Make the mince mixture into 4 patties (or 2 very large ones!) and place into the hot pot, cook on both sides until golden brown.
4. Assemble the burgers by spreading the mustard and mayonnaise onto one of the lettuce leaves, place the patty on top, place the cheese on top of the patty, then place 2 slices of beetroot and 2 pickles on top of the cheese, place the other lettuce leaf on top.
5. Devour and enjoy!

Crumbed Pork and Ginger Rice with Bok Choi

Tender morsels of crumbed pork, gingery-garlic rice, fresh bok choi with a drizzle of soy sauce. Your loved one will be forever grateful to you if you place this incredible dish in front of them!

Time: approximately 45 minutes

Ingredients:
- 14 oz pork meat, cut into strips
- 1 egg, lightly beaten
- 1 cup breadcrumbs, tossed with some salt and pepper
- ¾ cup dry basmati rice
- 1 ½ cups (12fl oz) chicken stock
- 1 tbsp grated fresh ginger
- 3 garlic cloves, finely chopped
- 1 knob of butter
- Olive oil
- 2 bunches of bok choi, ends removed
- 2 tbsp soy sauce
- ½ tsp sesame oil

Method:
1. Dip the pork strips into the beaten egg, then transfer them straight into the breadcrumbs, toss them in the crumbs until coated, set aside.
2. Add the rice, chicken stock, ginger, garlic, and butter to the Instant Pot and stir to combine, press the RICE button, secure the lid onto the pot, and allow the rice to cook automatically (the pot will figure out the cook time for you!).
3. Once the pot beeps, quick-release the pressure and remove the lid, fluff the rice before spooning into a bowl and setting aside.
4. Rinse out the inner pot and replace it back into the Instant Pot.
5. Add a drizzle of olive oil into the pot and press the SAUTE button, adjust the temperature to HIGH.
6. Once the oil is hot, add the pork strips to the pot and sauté until golden and crispy on all sides, set aside.
7. Pour 1 cup of water into the pot (no need to rinse the pot out this time) and place the steaming basket into the pot, place the bok choi into the basket.

8. Secure the lid onto the pot and press the STEAM button, adjust the time to 3 minutes.

9. Once the pot beeps, quick-release the pressure and remove the lid.

10. Divide the rice into two bowls, divide the pork and place on top of the rice, and finally place the bok choi on top of the pork and drizzle with soy sauce and sesame oil.

Poultry

For one simple bird, chicken really does offer a whole world of meal possibilities. Here you will find ideas for chicken thighs, breasts, drumsticks, and the whole bird.

White Wine Chicken Breasts on Creamy Polenta

White wine, cream, and rosemary generously drizzled over tender chicken breasts, on a bed of creamy polenta. It might sound a bit fancy, (and it tastes fancy too!) but it's actually super easy and quick to create. Oh, I should add...there's a bit of cream and butter in this dish, so it's best as a treat!

Time: approximately 40 minutes

Ingredients:
- Olive oil
- 2 chicken breasts, skinless
- 1 cup (8fl oz) chicken stock (for the chicken breasts)
- ½ cup (4fl oz) dry white wine
- 1 cup (8fl oz) heavy cream
- 1 sprig fresh rosemary
- 4 garlic cloves, finely chopped
- Salt and pepper, to taste
- 1 cup (8fl oz) milk
- 1 cup (8fl oz) chicken stock (for the polenta)
- 1 cup instant polenta
- 1 knob of butter

Method:
1. Drizzle some olive oil into the Instant Pot and press the SAUTE button, adjust the temperature to HIGH.
2. Once the oil is hot, add the chicken breasts to the pot and sauté for about 2 minutes on each side until golden and crispy.
3. Add the stock, wine, cream, rosemary, garlic, salt, and pepper to the pot and stir to combine.
4. Secure the lid onto the pot and press the POULTRY button, keep the time at the default 15 minutes.
5. Once the pot beeps, quick-release the pressure and remove the lid.
6. For the polenta: you can either remove the chicken and sauce from the Instant Pot and use it to cook the polenta on the SAUTE button if you wish, or you could simply use a pot on the stove to cook the polenta while the chicken cooks. Simply pour the milk and stock into a pot and bring to a simmer. Pour the polenta into the pot as

you whisk continuously. Keep whisking the polenta until it becomes thick and creamy. Add the butter, salt, and pepper and stir to combine.

7. Place a good dollop of polenta onto a plate and place a chicken breast on top, pour over a generous amount of white wine sauce before serving!

Honey-Glazed Cashew Chicken Drumsticks

Honey, salted cashews, and chicken drumsticks are a surprisingly delicious trio. Serve with a fresh salad and some crispy roasted potatoes. Make extra so you can have a cold drumstick for a snack or light lunch the next day!

Time: approximately 25 minutes

Ingredients:
- 8 chicken drumsticks (2 each for dinner, then 2 each for lunch the next day)
- 4 garlic cloves, crushed
- 3 tbsp honey
- 3 tbsp soy sauce
- 1 cup (8fl oz) chicken stock
- 1/3 cup roasted, salted cashew nuts, roughly chopped

Method:
1. Place the drumsticks, garlic, honey, soy sauce, and chicken stock into the Instant Pot, stir to combine and coat the drumsticks.
2. Secure the lid onto the pot and press the POULTRY button, keep the time at the default 15 minutes.
3. Once the pot beeps, quick-release the pressure and remove the lid.
4. Serve the drumsticks with a drizzle of honey/soy liquid and a sprinkling of crushed cashew nuts.

Roast Chicken for Dinner and Leftovers

A whole roast chicken can serve two people for a generous dinner, and lunches for a couple of days. In the Summer-time I serve with crispy salad and buttered bread, and in the Winter-time I serve with roasted root veggies and peas.

Time: approximately 45 minutes

Ingredients:
- 4 garlic cloves, skin on, crushed with the back of a knife
- 1 onion, skin on, cut into quarters
- 1 lemon, cut in half
- 2 cups (16fl oz) chicken stock
- 1 whole chicken
- 1 tbsp butter
- 1 tsp dried mixed herbs
- Salt, to taste

Method:
1. Place the crushed garlic cloves, onion quarters and lemon halves into the Instant Pot, pour the chicken stock over top.
2. Place the chicken on top of the lemon and onions.
3. Rub the top of the chicken with the butter, then sprinkle with the dried herbs and salt.
4. Secure the lid onto the pot and press the POULTRY button, adjust the time to 30 minutes.
5. Once the pot beeps, allow the pot to release naturally before you remove the lid.
6. OPTIONAL STEP: heat a frying pan before you remove the chicken from the pot. Place the chicken into the hot pot and fry on all sides for a couple of minutes until the skin is golden and crispy.
7. You can use any leftover liquid in the pot to make gravy by removing the lemon and onion, adding about 2 teaspoons of plain flour and stirring until a thick sauce forms.
8. Use the leftover chicken carcass to make homemade stock by boiling the carcass in a large pot with enough water to cover the carcass. Add onions, carrots, and celery to flavor the stock, (boil for as long as you can, at least 3 hours). Drain through a sieve before using or storing.

Chicken and Mushroom Pies

These pies only have a small amount of pastry as a topping, so they are a bit healthier than other pastry-encased pies. Classic flavors of chicken, mushroom, and herbs work together seamlessly. You will need 2 one-person pie tins.

Time: approximately 50 minutes

Ingredients:
- 14 oz chicken thighs, boneless and skinless, cut into small pieces
- 1 onion, finely chopped
- 3 garlic cloves, finely chopped
- 2 large Portobello mushrooms
- ½ cup (4fl oz) dry white wine
- ½ cup (4fl oz) heavy cream
- ½ tsp dried mixed herbs
- Salt and pepper, to taste
- Small amount of butter
- Store-bought puff pastry (you don't need much at all, just 2 circles to cover the pies)

Method:
1. Place the chicken, onion, garlic, mushrooms, wine, cream, herbs, salt, and pepper into the Instant Pot, stir to combine.
2. Secure the lid onto the pot and press the MEAT/STEW button, adjust the time to 20 minutes.
3. Once the pot beeps, quick-release the pressure and remove the lid, stir the mixture.
4. Preheat the oven to 374 degrees Fahrenheit and grease 2 pie tins with butter.
5. Place the tins face-down onto a sheet of pastry and cut around the edge of the tin to create a circle to fit neatly on top of the pie.
6. Divide the chicken mixture into the two tins and then place the pastry rounds on top.
7. Cut 4 little slits into the pastry and place the pies into the oven.
8. Bake for about 25 minutes or until the pastry is golden and the mixture is bubbling underneath.
9. Serve with fresh greens!

Chicken and Pesto Spaghetti

Pasta is so affordable, filling, and delicious. I love to make this incredibly tasty chicken and pesto spaghetti when I can't be bothered putting much effort into dinner but I want to serve something impressive and yummy.

Time: approximately 20 minutes

Ingredients:
- Olive oil
- 3 chicken thighs, boneless and skinless, cut into small pieces
- 7 oz dried spaghetti
- 3 garlic cloves, finely chopped
- 2 cups (8fl oz) chicken stock
- 2 tbsp store-bought basil pesto
- Parmesan cheese

Method:
1. Drizzle some olive oil into the Instant Pot and press the SAUTE button, keep the temperature at NORMAL.
2. Add the chicken to the hot pot and sauté for a couple of minutes to brown and pre-cook slightly.
3. Add the spaghetti, garlic, stock, and 1 cup of water to the pot.
4. Secure the lid onto the pot and press the POULTRY button, adjust the time to 10 minutes.
5. Once the pot beeps, quick-release the pressure and remove the lid.
6. Stir the pesto through the pasta and add a pinch of salt and pepper.
7. Serve immediately, with a sprinkling of grated Parmesan cheese!

Chili Ginger Chicken with Peanuts and Coriander

There are many strong flavors in this tasty dish. Ginger and coriander give an Asian attitude, chili provides the hit of heat, and peanuts give a crunch to die for. This recipe uses chicken thighs, but you could swap them for drumsticks if you wish!

Time: approximately 20 minutes

Ingredients:
- 4 chicken thighs, boneless, skinless
- 4 garlic cloves, finely chopped
- 1 fresh red chili, finely chopped
- 1 tbsp grated fresh ginger
- 1 cup (8fl oz) chicken stock
- Salt and pepper, to taste
- ¼ cup roasted, salted peanuts, roughly chopped
- Handful of fresh coriander, finely chopped

Method:
1. Place the chicken, garlic, chili, ginger, stock, salt, and pepper into the Instant Pot, stir to combine.
2. Secure the lid onto the pot and press the POULTRY button, keep the time at the default 15 minutes.
3. Once the pot beeps, quick-release the pressure and remove the lid.
4. Serve the chicken with a drizzle of leftover liquid, and sprinkle the peanuts and fresh coriander over the top.
5. This dish is lovely when served with plain rice or polenta.

Chicken Meatballs with Creamy Mushroom and Wine Sauce

Minced chicken gets overlooked, but it's so yummy when made into burger patties, dumplings, or in this case, meatballs! Creamy mushroom sauce adds another layer of flavor and texture. I like to serve with buttered noodles or some simple greens if I'm trying to be a bit healthier.

Time: approximately 30 minutes

Ingredients:
- 14 oz minced chicken
- 1 onion, finely chopped
- 4 garlic cloves, finely chopped
- 1 egg, lightly beaten
- ½ cup breadcrumbs
- ½ tsp dried mixed herbs
- Salt and pepper, to taste
- Olive oil
- ½ cup dry white wine
- 4 large Portobello mushrooms, sliced
- 1 cup cream
- ½ chicken stock cube
- ½ tsp dried rosemary

Method:
1. Mix together the minced chicken, onion, garlic, egg, breadcrumbs, herbs, salt, and pepper in a large bowl.
2. Roll the mixture into balls (about the size of a golf ball, but hey, you know what a meatball looks like!) and set aside.
3. Drizzle some olive oil into your Instant Pot and press the SAUTE button, keep the temperature at NORMAL.
4. Once the oil is hot, place the meatballs into the pot and cook for a few minutes to brown and seal the outside of the balls.
5. Add the wine to the pot and cook for a couple of minutes to burn off the alcohol.
6. Add the mushrooms, cream, stock cube, and rosemary to the pot.
7. Secure the lid onto the pot and press the POULTRY button and keep the time at the default 15 minutes.
8. Once the pot beeps, quick-release the pressure and remove the lid.
9. Serve your meatballs and creamy mushrooms with pasta, salad, roasted veggies... anything you feel like!

Chicken and Chickpea Salad

Chickpeas are like little nuggets of filling, fiber-filled goodness. Lemon-drizzled chicken, fresh parsley, crispy lettuce, and salty bites of feta make a unique and yummy salad. I like to make this for a filling lunch on busy days.

Time: approximately 25 minutes

Ingredients:
- 1 cup (8fl oz) chicken stock
- 2 chicken breasts, sliced into quarters (lengthways)
- 1 lemon, cut into slices
- 1 tin chickpeas (approximately 10oz more or less), drained and rinsed
- Handful of fresh parsley, finely chopped
- ½ iceberg lettuce, roughly chopped
- 5 oz feta cheese, cut into small chunks or cubes
- 2 tbsp pine nuts, toasted on a dry fry pan until golden
- Salt and pepper, to taste
- 1 tbsp apple cider vinegar or balsamic vinegar (for the dressing, choose the one you like best)
- Olive oil

Method:
1. Pour the chicken stock into your Instant Pot, then place the chicken breast pieces into the pot.
2. Lay the lemon slices on top of the chicken (don't worry if they fall off the chicken, their juices and flavor will still infuse the meat by being in the pot).
3. Secure the lid onto the pot and press the POULTRY button, keep the time at the default 15 minutes.
4. Once the pot beeps, quick-release the pressure and remove the lid.
5. Place the chicken pieces onto a board to rest while you prepare the rest of the salad.
6. In a salad bowl, place the chickpeas, parsley, lettuce, feta, pine nuts, salt, and pepper, toss to combine.
7. Slice the chicken into pieces and add to the salad.
8. Mix your chosen vinegar with olive oil, little bits at a time until you reach the desired taste. Some people prefer an oilier dressing, while others like a stronger vinegar flavor, so go with your taste.

Moroccan-Stuffed Chicken Breasts with Couscous

If you have a good butcher close to where you live or work, then make use of it by buying the exact amount of meat you need for you and your other half. These chicken breasts are stuffed with Moroccan-inspired spices, and apricots.

Time: approximately 45 minutes

Ingredients:
- 1 onion, finely chopped
- 1 tsp ground cinnamon
- 1 tsp ground cumin
- ½ ground paprika
- ½ tsp ground ginger
- ½ cup dried apricots, finely chopped
- Salt and pepper, to taste
- 2 chicken breasts, sliced lengthways to create a pocket
- Olive oil
- 1 tin chopped tomatoes
- 1 ½ cups chicken stock
- 1 cup dried instant couscous
- Small knob of butter (about 2tsp but it doesn't need to be exact)

Method:
1. Prepare the chicken filling by combining the onions, cinnamon, cumin, paprika, ginger, apricots, salt, and pepper in a small bowl.
2. Place your chicken breasts on a board (they should be sliced lengthways to reveal a pocket, don't cut them completely in half, just create a slit so you can fill the breast neatly) and rub with olive oil, salt, and pepper.
3. Divide the stuffing mixture between the two chicken breasts and tightly stuff.
4. If you like, you can press 2 toothpicks into the opening of each chicken breast to keep them tightly closed.
5. Drizzle some olive oil into the Instant Pot and press the SAUTE button, adjust the temperature to HIGH.
6. Once the pot is hot, place the chicken breasts into the pot and sauté on both sides for a few minutes until each side is golden brown.
7. Pour the tinned tomatoes into the pot with the chicken and add a sprinkle of salt and pepper.

8. Secure the lid onto the pot and press the POULTRY button, adjust the time to 30 minutes.

9. As the chicken cooks, prepare the couscous: place the chicken stock into a pot and bring to the boil. Once the stock is boiling, pour the couscous into the pot and immediately turn off the heat and place the lid onto the pot. Leave the couscous in the pot as the chicken cooks. It will cook and become fluffy and soft!

10. Once the Instant Pot beeps, quick-release the pressure and remove the chicken breasts from the pot and place on a board to rest.

11. Take the lid off the couscous pot and sprinkle with salt and pepper, add the knob of butter and fluff the couscous with a fork, the butter will melt into the couscous.

12. Serve the chicken breasts on a bed of buttery couscous.

13. You can either discard the leftover tomatoes in the pot, or you could use them to create a nice sauce by adding herbs, balsamic vinegar, and a touch of chili and simmering until thick and rich.

Mexican-Inspired Chicken Soup

Lime, chili, coriander, and black beans are some of the best flavors ever, in my opinion. This Mexican-inspired chicken soup is perfect for 2, and if you're lucky, there may even be leftovers to devour for lunch!

Time: approximately 40 minutes

Ingredients:
- 4 boneless, skinless chicken thighs, cut into about 5 pieces each
- 1 onion, finely chopped
- 4 garlic cloves, finely chopped
- 2 limes
- 1 fresh red chili, finely chopped
- Large handful of fresh coriander roughly chopped and split into two (half for the soup, half for garnishing)
- 32fl oz chicken stock
- 1 tin black beans, drained and rinsed (about 10oz once drained but honestly it doesn't matter if there's more or less)
- Salt and pepper, to taste
- 8fl oz cream

Method:
1. Place the chicken, onions, garlic, juice of both limes, red chili, half of the coriander, chicken stock, black beans, salt, and pepper into your Instant Pot and stir to combine.
2. Secure the lid onto the pot and press the SOUP button, keep the time to the default 30 minutes.
3. Once the pot beeps, quick-release the pressure, remove the lid, and give the soup a good stir.
4. Stir the cream through the soup before serving with a big pile of fresh cilantro on top.
5. Oh, and a few tortilla chips on the side wouldn't go astray!

Broccoli, Pea, Parmesan, and Chicken One-Pot Dinner

...,ore you skip this recipe (I know that peas are not a very popular vegetable for many people!) just remember that you can leave the peas out, or replace them with another veggie. But, as a pea-lover, I had to add at least one pea-filled recipe!

Time: approximately 40 minutes

Ingredients:
- Olive oil
- 4 boneless, skinless chicken thighs
- 2 cups frozen peas
- ½ head of broccoli, chopped into florets
- 16fl oz chicken stock
- ¾ cup basmati rice
- Salt and pepper, to taste
- ½ cup grated parmesan cheese

Method:
1. Drizzle some olive oil into the Instant Pot and press the SAUTE button, adjust the temperature to HIGH.
2. Once the pot is hot, add the chicken to the pot and sauté for about 3 minutes until the chicken is golden. Note: this step is not crucial, you don't need to pre-brown the chicken but I prefer to do this.
3. Add the peas, broccoli, stock, rice, salt, and pepper to the pot and stir to combine.
4. Secure the lid onto the pot and press the POULTRY button, adjust the time to 30 minutes.
5. Once the pot beeps, allow the pressure to release naturally, this will help to ensure the rice is cooked and fluffy.
6. Sprinkle with Parmesan cheese
7. Please note: the broccoli in this dish will be very soft, which some people don't like, so if you prefer crunchier broccoli you can steam it separately and serve it on the side!
8. I hope you like this slightly odd dish... I promise it's tasty!

Chicken and Avocado Burgers

Chicken and avocado burgers are quite possibly one of the most popular non-beef burgers ever. Choose some lovely, fresh buns (brioche buns if you can!) and add any extra fillings you and your loved one like.

Time: approximately 30 minutes

Ingredients:
- 1 large chicken breast, sliced in half lengthways (to create two thin filets)
- Olive oil
- ½ tsp Cajun seasoning (or a mixture of your favorite spices, but Cajun is so yummy in this burger)
- Salt and pepper, to taste
- 2 burger buns
- 1 avocado, sliced
- Any other toppings you like: mayo, ketchup, lettuce, tomatoes, red onion, pickles, camembert, cranberry sauce – or simply keep them plain!

Method:
1. Rub the chicken breasts with olive oil, Cajun seasoning, salt, and pepper.
2. Press the SAUTE button on your Instant Pot and adjust the temperature to HIGH.
3. Once the pot is hot, place the chicken filets into the pot and sauté on both sides until cooked through and just starting to char on the outside.
4. Place the chicken on a board to rest while you prepare the buns.
5. Slice the buns in half and (here's where it gets delicious) place them cut-side down into the Instant Pot (the SAUTE function on HIGH should still be on).
6. Allow the buns to heat and cook in the leftover chicken oil, about 3 minutes, or until they are hot and the cut sides are crispy and covered in chicken-flavored olive oil.
7. Assemble your burgers with lots of sliced avocado, your spiced chicken breast, and any other toppings you like best.

Lemon Chicken with Kale, Spinach, and Toasted Seed Salad

Another classic! This lemon chicken is so yummy you'll wish both portions were for you. The kale, spinach, and toasted seed salad is full of greens and healthy fats.

Time: approximately 40 minutes

Ingredients:
- 4 chicken drumsticks
- 12 oz chicken stock
- 1 sprig fresh rosemary
- Salt and pepper, to taste
- 2 lemons
- Olive oil
- About 6 large kale leaves, stalks removed, leaves cut or shredded into small pieces
- 2 tbsp pumpkin seeds
- 2 tbsp sunflower seeds
- 2 cups baby spinach leaves

Method:
1. Place chicken drumsticks, chicken stock, rosemary, salt, pepper, the juice of both the lemons, then place the squeezed lemon halves into the pot as well (extra flavor please!).
2. Secure the lid onto the pot and press the POULTRY button, adjust the time to 30 minutes.
3. While the chicken is cooking, prepare the salad: heat a frying pan with a small amount of olive oil over a medium heat.
4. Place the chopped kale into the hot fry pan with a pinch of salt, sauté until just beginning to wilt, transfer the kale to salad bowl and keep the pan on the heat.
5. Add the pumpkin and sunflower seeds to the hot pan and keep jiggling the pan as they toast, as soon as you smell the toasted aroma and the seeds begin to turn brown, toss them straight into the salad bowl with the kale. Add the spinach to the bowl and toss together with a swig of olive oil.
6. Once the Instant Pot beeps, quick-release the pressure, remove the lid, and place the chicken drumsticks on a plate with a generous spoonful of leftover lemony liquid.
7. Serve with your beautiful green, seed-filled salad.

Seafood

Impress your other half with a light and elegant fish or seafood meal. I find that fish is the best protein to use when I'm trying to eat a bit lighter and healthier, so if that sounds like you too...then take a look through this section for some yummy ideas.

White Fish Curry for Two, with Banana and Coconut Side Dish

I love fish curry, it's so delicate and light, yet feels like a comfort food at the same time. My Mum always serves curry with a cooling side dish made from sliced bananas, dried coconut, and lemon juice – it cuts through the heat and adds a dash of sweetness to the dish.

Time: approximately 30 minutes

Ingredients:
- 4 tbsp store-bought curry paste (it's not cheating if it's a high-quality paste!)
- 12 oz fresh white fish (use any kind you can find as long as it's fresh), cut into chunks
- 12 oz coconut milk
- 8 oz fish stock
- 1 lime
- Salt and pepper, to taste
- Fresh coriander, roughly chopped
- 1 large banana, peeled and sliced
- 2 tbsp desiccated or shredded coconut
- 1 lemon

Method:
1. Press the SAUTE button on your Instant Pot and adjust the temperature to HIGH.
2. Add the curry paste to the hot pot and heat until fragrant.
3. Add the fish, coconut milk, stock, juice of 1 lime, salt, and pepper to the pot and stir to combine.
4. Secure the lid onto the pot and press the SOUP button, adjust the time to 20 minutes.
5. While the curry cooks, prepare the banana coconut side dish: place the sliced bananas, coconut, and juice of one lemon into a small bowl, stir to combine.
6. Once the Instant Pot beeps, quick-release the pressure and remove the lid.
7. Serve the curry on its own, or with rice and/or naan, with freshly chopped coriander, and of course, the banana and coconut side dish.

Smoked Fish Pots

You will need some individual ramekins or one-person deep pie dishes for this recipe. Flaked smoked fish, eggs, parsley, and a slice of toast – a simple (and slightly old-fashioned!) supper for 2.

Ingredients:
- 1 tbsp butter, melted
- 14 oz smoked fish (smoked trout is lovely, but any fish works)
- 3 eggs, lightly beaten
- 4fl oz milk
- ½ tsp baking powder
- Handful of fresh parsley, finely chopped
- Salt and pepper, to taste
- 2 slices of thick bread (sure, this is optional...but buttered toast goes so well with these smoky pots!)
- A few slices of lemon wedges

Method:
1. Grease your ramekins or individual pie dishes with butter.
2. Flake the smoked fish with a fork and place the fish into a bowl.
3. Add the eggs, milk, baking powder, parsley, salt, and pepper to the fish bowls.
4. Pour 2 cups of water into your Instant Pot and place a trivet or rack into the pot.
5. Place the filled smoked fish pots onto the trivet or rack (above the water), secure the lid onto the pot, press the STEAM button, and adjust the time to 10 minutes.
6. Once the pot beeps, quick-release the pressure and remove the lid.
7. The fish pots will be very hot so be careful when removing them from the Instant Pot.
8. Serve with hot, buttered toast and a wedge of lemon.

Orange-Glazed Steamed Salmon

When I first made this dish, I was surprised at how delicious it was, as I'm usually a bit skeptical about fruity flavors with savory dishes. The orange glaze is sticky, sweet, and subtle.

Time: approximately 15 minutes

Ingredients:
- 2 fresh oranges
- 1 tbsp honey
- 1 tbsp soy sauce
- 2 salmon filets, skin on, bones removed, seasoned with a pinch of salt and pepper

Method:
1. Squeeze the juice of both oranges into a pot and add the honey and soy sauce, (you could use your Instant Pot on the SAUTE function, but honestly, I find it easier to just use a small pot on the stove for this glaze).
2. Place the pot over a low heat and bring the mixture to a simmer, leave to gently simmer for about 7 minutes as you prepare the salmon. The glaze will thicken slightly and will become sticky.
3. Pour 2 cups of water into the Instant Pot and place the steaming basket into the pot.
4. Place the salmon filets into the basket and secure the lid onto the pot.
5. Press the STEAM button and adjust the time to 3 minutes (this will result in a lightly-cooked salmon).
6. Once the pot beeps, quick-release the steam and remove the lid.
7. Take the salmon filets out of the basket and place them into the pot of hot orange glaze, spoon the glaze over the salmon so it's completed coated.
8. Serve the salmon with an extra drizzle of orange glaze over top.
9. Some serving ideas: mashed potatoes, fresh green beans, long-stemmed broccoli, or a simple fresh salad.

Fish Balls with Garlic Aioli Dip

The taste and texture of these fish balls resembles that of fish cakes, but they are daintier than fish cakes, and perfect to serve as a snack or starter for you and your pal. The garlic aioli dip is a perfect accompaniment because...well...garlic aioli!

Time: approximately 25 minutes

Ingredients:
- ½ cup plain aioli (or mayo if you don't have aioli)
- 1 garlic clove
- 1 lemon
- Salt and pepper, to taste
- 13 oz cooked or smoked fish of your choice
- 1 egg, lightly beaten1
- 1 cup bread crumbs
- 1 tbsp tomato puree
- 1 tsp paprika
- 1 tsp chili powder
- Handful of fresh cilantro finely chopped
- Olive oil

Method:
1. Prepare the garlic aioli by mixing the aioli or mayo with the crushed garlic clove, salt, pepper, and a squeeze of lemon in a small bowl. Have a taste and add more garlic if it's not garlicky enough, or a dash more aioli if it's a bit too garlicky for your taste.
2. Flake the cooked or smoked fish into a bowl, add the egg, bread crumbs, tomato puree, paprika, chili powder, fresh cilantro, salt, and pepper, stir to combine.
3. Drizzle plenty of olive oil into your Instant Pot and press the SAUTE button, adjust the temperature to HIGH.
4. Roll the fish mixture into golf ball-sized balls and add them to the hot pot.
5. Sauté the fish balls for about 10 minutes, turning every couple of minutes until they are golden and crispy all round.
6. Serve with some toothpicks for easy eating, lemon wedges, and your garlic aioli.

Calamari Linguine

Nothing too fancy here, the calamari speaks for itself. A simple sauce of butter, lemon, and herbs dresses this Summery, perfect-for-two dish.

Time: approximately 25 minutes

Ingredients:
- Olive oil
- 10 oz cleaned calamari (frozen is fine)
- 7 oz dried linguine
- 32fl oz chicken stock (you could use fish stock but I find chicken stock is nicer)
- ½ tsp chili flakes (you can leave this out, but I can't help putting chili in everything!)
- Salt and pepper, to taste
- 2 oz butter
- 1 lemon
- Small sprig of thyme, stalks removed, leaves finely chopped
- Small bunch of fresh parsley, finely chopped
- A few fresh oregano leaves, finely chopped

Method:
1. Drizzle some olive oil into the Instant Pot and press the SAUTE button, adjust the temperature to HIGH.
2. Place the calamari into the hot pot and sauté for about 5 minutes, stirring as they cook.
3. Place the linguini, chicken stock, chili, salt, and pepper into the pot and make sure all of the linguine is covered in stock.
4. Secure the lid onto the pot and press the MANUAL button, adjust the pressure to HIGH, and adjust the time to 8 minutes.
5. Once the pot beeps, quick-release the pressure and remove the lid, give the pasta a stir.
6. Place the butter, juice of one lemon, fresh herbs, salt, and pepper into the pot and leave for a couple of minutes to allow the butter to melt.
7. Serve immediately.

Buttered Prawns with Chili Dip

Again...butter. What is it with me and butter?! I find butter is one of the best ways to dress seafood (and everything else). These buttery prawns are divine when dipped into the spicy chilli dip with an oil and vinegar base.

Ingredients:
- Olive oil (for cooking the prawn)
- 6 oz prawns (frozen or raw)
- 3 garlic cloves, crushed
- 2 lb butter
- 1 fresh red chili, finely chopped
- 2 tbsp olive oil
- 1 tsp sesame oil
- 1 tbsp rice wine vinegar or apple cider vinegar
- 1 tsp sugar

Method:
1. Drizzle some olive oil into your Instant Pot and press the SAUTE button, keep the temperature at NORMAL.
2. Add the prawns and the garlic to the hot pot and sauté for about 5 minutes, stirring every minute.
3. Add the butter to the pot and stir as it melts into the prawns.
4. Once the butter has melted, allow the prawns to simmer in the buttery sauce for a further few minutes or until they are cooked to your liking (give one a taste and see).
5. Prepare the dipping sauce by mixing the chili, olive oil, sesame oil, vinegar, and sugar in a small bowl. Give the sauce a taste and add more of any ingredient until you reach the balance of flavors you desire (I like mine to be hot and vinegary, but you might like yours sweeter and oilier).
6. Use a slotted spoon to scoop the prawns from the Instant Pot and onto a serving plate or bowl, drizzle some extra butter sauce over the top before serving with the chili sauce on the side.

Tuna, Cheese, and Tomato Toasties (Fried Sandwiches!)

Can't face cooking a "proper" dinner? Make tuna toasties! These are actually really fun to make and eat with a partner or friend, as you can hang out in the kitchen together as you prepare the fillings and get your Instant Pot fired up.

Time: approximately 25 minutes

Ingredients:
- 4 slices of good-quality, thick-sliced bread
- Butter (for spreading on the outside of the toasties)
- 2 slices of cheddar, mozzarella, or Swiss cheese (use your yummiest cheese)
- 2 small tins of tuna (plain or flavored) drained
- Salt and pepper, to taste
- 1 large tomato, sliced

Method:
1. Press the SAUTE button on your Instant Pot and keep the temperature at NORMAL.
2. Prepare the bread by buttering each slice on one side (be generous with the butter, it will prevent the sandwiches from sticking).
3. With the buttered side of the bread on the outside, lay the bread on a board, ready to be filled.
4. Lay a slice of cheese onto two slices of bread (on the unbuttered side), place the tuna on top of the cheese (one tin per sandwich), lay a couple of tomato slices on top of the tuna then sprinkle with salt and pepper.
5. Lay the other slices of bread on top of each sandwich (buttered side up).
6. Carefully place the sandwiches into the hot pot and press down with a fish slice or spatula.
7. Cook for about 3 minutes before carefully flipping the sandwiches over and cooking the other side until both sides are golden and crispy, and the cheese is melting out the sides.
8. Serve immediately (don't worry if it's messy, they're meant to be!).
9. Serving suggestions: salad, sweet potato oven fries, pickles.

Fish and Brown Rice One-Pot Wonder

Another one-pot dish you can rely on when you want to get dinner on the table quickly, with minimal dishes to face afterward. Use any fish you can buy, as long as it's fresh.

Time: approximately 20 minutes

Ingredients:
- Olive oil
- 1 onion, finely chopped
- 3 garlic cloves, finely chopped
- ½ tsp ground turmeric
- ½ tsp ground paprika
- ½ tsp ground chili
- 1 cup brown rice
- 20fl oz fish stock (just use chicken stock if you don't have fish stock)
- 2 fresh fish fillets, cut into large chunks
- Salt and pepper, to taste
- ½ cup plain yogurt
- Fresh mint leaves, finely chopped

Method:
1. Press the SAUTE button on your Instant Pot and keep the temperature at NORMAL, drizzle some olive oil into the pot.
2. Add the onion, garlic, turmeric, paprika, and chili to the hot pot and sauté for a couple of minutes until the onions are soft.
3. Add the rice and stir to coat in the oil and spices.
4. Pour the stock into the pot and stir to combine.
5. Place the fish pieces carefully into the pot and sprinkle some salt and pepper over top.
6. Secure the lid onto the pot and press the RICE function, leave the pot to cook automatically.
7. Once the pot beeps, quick-release the pressure and remove the lid.
8. The rice should be cooked and the fish should be flaky and well cooked too.
9. Serve with a dollop of plain yogurt and a sprinkling of fresh mint.

Steamed Fish and Green Veggies

This one is for when you've had a bit of a blowout over the weekend and you just need to eat an extremely clean and healthy dinner to get yourself (and your partner in crime) back on track...well, that's how it goes in my house anyway! Fish and greens is the ultimate health it: good fats, protein, and nutrients.

Time: approximately 20 minutes

Ingredients:
- ½ broccoli, cut into florets
- 1 cup chopped kale
- 1 cup green beans (fresh or frozen)
- 3 cups baby spinach leaves
- Salt and pepper, to taste
- 1 tsp sesame oil
- 2 fresh fish filets

Method:
1. Pour 2 cups of water into your Instant Pot and place the steaming basket into the pot.
2. Place the broccoli into the basket, then the kale, then the beans, then the spinach.
3. Sprinkle the greens with salt, pepper, and sesame oil.
4. Place the fish filets on top of the veggies and give them a sprinkle of salt and pepper.
5. Secure the lid onto the pot and press the STEAM button, manually adjust the time to 6 minutes.
6. Once the pot beeps, quick-release the pressure and remove the lid.
7. Serve the fish and veggies immediately.
8. If you feel a bit deprived of carbs with this dish, roast some sweet potatoes or butternut squash in the oven to bulk it out a bit!

Flaked Salmon Salad

Flaked cooked salmon, steamed new potatoes, asparagus, salad greens, and a mustard-based dressing – one of the nicest salad combinations ever. Add some boiled eggs if you're in need of extra protein!

Time: approximately 20 minutes

Ingredients:
- 6 new season potatoes, cut in half
- Salt and pepper, to taste
- 1 large salmon fillet
- Olive oil (for cooking)
- 8 spears of asparagus
- 1tbsp Dijon mustard
- 2 tbsp olive oil
- 1 tsp sugar
- 2 tbsp apple cider vinegar
- ½ iceberg lettuce, roughly shredded
- ½ cucumber, cut into small pieces
- 1 red capsicum, seeds removed, flesh sliced

Method:
1. Pour 2 cups of water into your Instant Pot and place the steaming basket into the pot.
2. Place the potatoes into the basket and sprinkle with salt, place the salmon filet on top of the potatoes.
3. Secure the lid onto the pot and press the STEAM button, manually adjust the time to 8 minutes.
4. While the potatoes and salmon are steaming, prepare the asparagus by heating some olive oil in a frying pan over a medium-high heat, place the asparagus into the pan and sprinkle with salt and pepper, sauté until they are soft but not mushy, take off from the heat and leave aside.
5. Once the Instant Pot beeps, quick-release the steam and remove the lid, place the basket of potatoes and salmon onto a board to cool as you prepare the rest of the salad.
6. Make the salad dressing by mixing together the mustard, olive oil, sugar, and vinegar in a small bowl, taste and adjust any ingredients to suit your tastes.

7. Place the lettuce, cucumber, and capsicum in a large salad bowl.
8. Place the cooled (but still warm) potatoes and asparagus into the salad bowl
9. Flake the salmon with a fork and add to the salad bowl.
10. Drizzle the dressing over the salad before serving, and toss to coat and combine.
11. Serve with toasted sourdough.

Raw Salmon Rice Bowls

If you're a bit shy when it comes to raw fish then by all means, you can pan fry the salmon and carry on with the recipe as is. But if you're anything like me, you LOVE raw salmon and all its oily goodness. Salmon, sushi rice, pickled cucumbers. Amazing.

Ingredients:
- 1 cup sushi rice
- Pinch of salt
- ½ cucumber, cut into very thin strips with a potato peeler
- ½ tsp sugar
- 1 tbsp rice wine vinegar
- ½ cucumber, cut into thin sticks
- 1 carrot, peeled and cut into very thin sticks or strips
- 1 salmon fillet, thinly sliced
- 1 tbsp sesame seeds, toasted on a dry frying pan (no oil)
- 1 nori sheet, cut into 4 pieces (I use scissors, it works wonders)

Method:
1. Place the rice into your Instant Pot and add 2 cups of water and a pinch of salt.
2. Secure the lid onto the pot and press the RICE button, leave the pot to cook the rice automatically.
3. Prepare the pickled cucumbers by placing the cucumber strips, sugar, and rice wine vinegar in a small bowl, leave to soak as the rice cooks.
4. Once the pot beeps, quick-release the pressure and remove the lid, transfer the rice into two serving bowls (leave some behind for a leftover portion if there's too much rice for you both in one sitting).
5. Place a small pile of pickled cucumbers on top of the rice, to the side of the bowl, place the cucumber sticks next to the pickles, place the carrot sticks next to the cucumber, then place the salmon strips in the center of the bowl.
6. Garnish with the nori squares and toasted sesame seeds.
7. Avocado strips and Japanese mayonnaise would also be a creamy and yummy addition to this dish.

Tuna Penne "Casserole"

ᶠ tuna comes to the rescue once again! This time, it comes in the form of a ...ᵤ tuna pasta bake for hungry nights. Dried pasta and tinned tuna...for any students out there, this one's for you, as it's very easy on the wallet.

Time: approximately 25 minutes

Ingredients:
- Olive oil
- 1 onion, finely chopped
- 4 garlic cloves, finely chopped
- 10 oz tinned tuna, drained
- 2 cups (about 8 oz give or take) dried penne pasta
- ½ tsp dried mixed herbs
- 1 tin chopped tomatoes
- ½ cup (4fl oz) crème fraiche (or plain heavy cream for a cheaper option)
- Salt and pepper, to taste

Method:
1. Drizzle some olive oil into your Instant Pot and press the SAUTE button, keep the temperature at NORMAL.
2. Add the onions and garlic to the pot and sauté until soft.
3. Add the tuna, penne pasta, mixed herbs, tomatoes, 1 cup (8floz) of water, crème fraiche, salt, and pepper, stir to combine.
4. Secure the lid onto the pot and press the MEAT/STEW button, adjust the time to 20 minutes.
5. Once the pot beeps, quick-release the pressure and remove the lid.
6. Give the casserole a stir and serve with greens.

Vegan & Vegetarian

Even if you and your cooking buddy aren't vegan or vegetarian you will still love these recipes. When the budget gets a bit tight and meat is off the cards, these recipes can save the day, as they're not only tasty and healthy, but they're affordable too.

Coconut, Kidney bean, Corn, and Lime Nacho Bowls (V, VG)

Kidney beans are the unsung heroes of the tinned-food world. They have so much nutritional value, they're cheap, and they're super delicious. This recipe is one of my favorites because it incorporates some of my favorite flavors: coconut and lime! I hope you like it too.

Time: approximately 30 minutes

Ingredients:
- 1 tin red kidney beans, drained
- 8fl oz coconut milk
- 1 tin corn kernels, drained
- 1 onion, finely chopped
- 4 garlic cloves, finely chopped
- 1 tsp ground paprika
- 1 tsp chili powder
- 1 tsp ground cumin
- Salt and pepper, to taste
- 2 juicy limes, halved
- 1 lettuce
- 1 avocado, sliced
- Large handful of fresh coriander, roughly chopped
- Enough vegan corn chips for two people (I'll leave that up to your discretion!)

Method:
1. Place the beans, coconut milk, corn, onion, garlic, paprika, chili, cumin, salt, pepper, and zest of one lime into your Instant Pot, stir to combine.
2. Secure the lid onto the pot and press the BEAN/CHILLI button and adjust the time to 25 minutes.
3. Once the pot beeps, quick-release the pressure, remove the lid, and stir the mixture.
4. Place a generous serving of the bean mixture onto a wide bowl or plate, place a pile of lettuce to one side of the plate or bowl, add some avocado slices, a handful of chopped cilantro, 2 lime halves, and a handful of corn chips onto the plate (yup, it's a lot!).
5. One thing left to do: devour! Preferably with a Margarita.

Veggie Burgers (V)

These are not just any old veggie burgers, they are THE veggie burgers. Mushrooms, chickpeas, corn, cheese...and that's just the patty. Friday night burgers-for-two – vegetarian style.

Time: approximately 25 minutes

Ingredients:
- 1 tin chickpeas, drained
- 2 large Portobello mushrooms, finely chopped
- 1 onion, finely chopped
- 3 garlic cloves, finely chopped
- ½ cup corn kernels (tinned, frozen, or fresh)
- ½ cup grated mozzarella cheese
- 1 egg
- Salt and pepper, to taste
- Herbs and spices of your choice
- Olive oil
- 2 burger buns
- Mustard
- Mayonnaise
- Lettuce
- Tomato
- 2 slices of cheddar (or any other melt-friendly cheese)

Method:
1. Mash the chickpeas in a bowl until they resemble a paste with a few lumps and chunks.
2. Add the mushroom pieces, onion, garlic, corn, mozzarella, egg, salt, and pepper to the bowl and stir to combine.
3. Now you can add any herbs and spices you like. Personally, I like paprika and chili (my usual spice duo!), but fresh parsley and thyme would be great too.
4. Drizzle some olive oil into your Instant Pot and press the SAUTE button, keep the temperature at NORMAL.
5. Shape your patty mixture into burgers (don't worry if it's rather sticky or difficult to shape, rugged patties are the best patties).
6. Place the patties into the hot pot and fry on both sides until golden and crispy.

7. To warm the buns, you can slice them in half and lay them sliced-side down in the Instant Pot on the SAUTE function once the patties have finished cooking.

8. The buns will soak up some of the yummy oil and flavors leftover from the patties.

9. Spread the buns with mustard and mayo, place a patty on top, then load up with lettuce, tomato, cheese, and any other tasty fillings you like (ahem, pickles...).

10. Eat messily and enjoy!

Corn, Mango, and Toasted Seed Tacos (V)

I've said it before (many times) and I will say it again, I'm usually against fruits (except citrus) in savory dishes...unless it's MANGO! Mango makes any taco a hundred times yummier. These tacos are filled with mango, corn, avocado, seeds, and a coriander-yoghurt crema.

Time: approximately 25 minutes

Ingredients:
- ½ cup (4fl oz) plain yogurt
- Handful of fresh coriander, finely chopped
- Olive oil
- 1 onion, finely chopped
- 1 tin corn kernels, drained
- 1 tin black beans, drained
- Salt and pepper, to taste
- 2 tbsp pumpkin seeds
- 2 tbsp sunflower seeds
- 4 flour tortillas (2 each)
- 4 tbsp refried beans (store bought, I like the ones with the adobo chili!)
- 1 avocado, sliced
- 1 fresh mango, peeled, flesh cut into small chunks

Method:
1. Prepare the crema by mixing the yogurt and coriander together (easy!).
2. Drizzle some olive oil into your Instant Pot and add the onion, corn, black beans, salt, pepper, and about 4floz of water.
3. Secure the lid onto the pot and press the MANUAL button, cook on HIGH for 10 minutes.
4. As the beans and corn are cooking, heat a small frying pan without any oil and toast the seeds until they are fragrant and beginning to turn golden.
5. Once the pot beeps, quick-release the pressure and remove the lid, stir the corn and bean mixture.
6. If you want to heat your tortillas, do it now by throwing them in the pan you used to toast the seeds and heat until they start to puff up.
7. Lay the tortillas on a board and spread thinly with refried beans.
8. Pile some of the corn and bean mixture on top (yup, 2 layers of beans!).

9. Add some avocado slices, then the mango (lots), sprinkle the toasted seeds on top, then drizzle with crema.

10. Serve with sangria for two!

Ramen Noodle Salad with Tofu, Peanuts and Avocado (V, VG)

I like to use avocado in vegetarian dishes as it provides an oily, fatty goodness as well as fiber and a great texture. Peanuts give awesome crunch, and tofu holds flavor and adds lots of protein. And the ramen noodles? They're there to provide moreish yumminess.

Time: approximately 15 minutes

Ingredients:

- 2 blocks of ramen (or 3 if you want a larger meal)
- Olive oil
- 5 oz firm tofu, cut into small cubes
- 1 tsp sesame oil
- 1 tbsp soy sauce
- 1 tsp Sriracha (chili sauce, or use 1tsp ground chili)
- 1 avocado, cut into chunks
- ¼ cup roasted, salted peanuts

Method:

1. Place the ramen noodle blocks into a bowl and cover with boiling water, cover the bowl and leave the noodles to cook as you prepare the rest (if your brand of noodle specifies different cooking methods then just follow those).
2. Drizzle some olive oil into the Instant Pot and press the SAUTE button, keep the temperature at NORMAL.
3. Place the tofu, sesame oil, soy sauce, and Sriracha into the hot pot and stir to coat and combine, sauté for about 7 minutes or until the tofu is golden and starting to char.
4. Drain the cooked noodles and add them to the pot, stir to combine and coat in sauce and seasoning.
5. Transfer the contents of the pot into a salad bowl and place the avocado chunks, peanuts, and any other additions you like on top (coriander, lime, extra chilli, grated carrot, cucumber pickles would all be great additions).
6. This salad is just as good when served cold.

Feta and Olive Spaghetti with Rosemary Ricotta (V)

This double-cheese spaghetti is for lovers of salty, briny flavors as the olives and feta cheese really tingle the taste buds. Serve with a glass of red wine, sit back, and relax with your friend or partner – this is definitely "couch in front of the TV" food.

Time: approximately 15 minutes

Ingredients:
- 7 oz dried spaghetti
- 30fl oz vegetable stock (enough to just cover the spaghetti)
- 10 black olives, stones removed, cut into small chunks
- 3 garlic cloves, finely chopped
- ½ tsp chili flakes
- Pepper, to taste
- 3 oz ricotta cheese
- 1 tsp chopped fresh rosemary
- 3 oz feta cheese, crumbled or cut into small chunks

Method:
1. Place the spaghetti, stock, olives, garlic, chili, and pepper (I don't add extra salt yet as the feta and olives are salty) into your Instant Pot and make sure the spaghetti is submerged in liquid.
2. Secure the lid onto the pot and press the MANUAL button, cook at a high pressure at 8 minutes.
3. Once the pot beeps, quick-release the pressure and remove the lid, stir the pasta.
4. Add the ricotta, rosemary, and feta to the pot and stir to combine, the pasta will be thick and creamy.
5. Taste to check if you need to add any extra salt, pepper, or chili if you want some heat.

Spinach and Ricotta Balls with Tomato Sauce (V)

Another use of ricotta cheese, this time with spinach and rich tomato sauce. This is lovely when served over polenta or pasta.

Time: approximately 18 minutes

Ingredients:
- 3 cups baby spinach, finely chopped
- 8 oz ricotta cheese
- ½ cup grated cheddar cheese
- Salt and pepper, to taste
- ¼ tsp grated nutmeg
- 1 egg
- Olive oil
- 4fl oz red wine
- 4 garlic cloves, finely chopped
- 16fl oz tomato passata
- 1 tsp sugar
- ½ tsp chili flakes
- 1 tsp vinegar (apple cider vinegar, malt vinegar, or red wine vinegar)

Method:
1. Mix together the chopped spinach, ricotta cheese, grated cheddar, salt, pepper, nutmeg, and egg in a large bowl, keep mixing until completely combined.
2. Drizzle some olive oil into your Instant Pot and press the SAUTE button, keep the temperature at NORMAL.
3. Add the garlic and red wine to the pot and sauté for about 3 minutes until the alcohol evaporates from the wine.
4. Add the tomato passata, sugar, chili flakes, vinegar, salt, and pepper, stir to combine.
5. Scoop the spinach and ricotta mixture with a spoon and shape into balls, place them into the pot, sitting on top/in the tomato mixture.
6. Once all of the mixture has been shaped into balls and added to the pot, secure the lid onto the pot and press the MANUAL button, cook on HIGH pressure for 10 minutes.
7. Once the pot beeps, quick-release the pressure, remove the lid, and serve the ricotta balls with a generous spoonful of rich tomato sauce.
8. Serve with any starches you like such as bread, pasta, or even roasted potatoes.

Tofu Satay with Fried Cauliflower Rice (V, VG)

Squares of firm tofu doused in peanut satay sauce, on a bed of fried cauliflower rice, this is a dream meal for anyone, not just those who follow a vegan or vegetarian diet!

Time: approximately 25 minutes

Ingredients:
- Olive oil
- ½ head of cauliflower, blitzed in a food processor until it resembles rice
- Salt and pepper, to taste
- 1 onion, finely chopped
- 3 garlic cloves, finely chopped
- 2 tsp brown sugar
- 1 tbsp soy sauce
- ½ cup crunchy vegan peanut butter
- 8fl oz coconut milk
- 7 oz firm tofu, cut into cubes

Method:
1. Drizzle some olive oil into you Instant Pot and press the SAUTE button, keep the temperature at NORMAL.
2. Add the cauliflower to the pot and add a generous sprinkle of salt and pepper.
3. Stir as the cauliflower fries and becomes cooked, golden, and slightly crispy.
4. Remove the cooked cauliflower from the pot and place in a covered bowl to keep warm as you prepare the satay tofu.
5. Add some more olive oil to the pot and add the onion and garlic, sauté for a few minutes until the onions are soft.
6. Add the sugar, soy sauce, peanut butter, and coconut milk, stir as the mixture comes to a simmer and the peanut butter melts into the mixture.
7. Add the tofu cubes and stir to coat them in sauce.
8. Secure the lid onto the pot and press the MANUAL button, cook on HIGH pressure for 6 minutes.
9. Once the pot beeps, quick-release the pressure and remove the lid.
10. Serve the tofu and satay sauce on top of a generous pile of fried cauliflower rice.

Slow-Cooked Sweet Potato Soup (V, VG)

Easy, creamy, filling, tasty. By slow-cooking on a low heat all day, the sweet potatoes become infused with onion, garlic, and spices. Pile the ingredients into the pot in the morning and come home after work to dinner. All you have to do is blitz the soup with a hand-held blender before serving.

Time: approximately 8 hours

Ingredients:
- 18 oz sweet potato, cut into chunks (peel if you like, but I keep the skin on)
- 1 onion, finely chopped
- 6 garlic cloves, finely chopped
- 28fl oz vegetable stock
- Salt and pepper, to taste
- 8fl oz coconut cream

Method:
1. Place the sweet potato, onion, garlic, stock, salt, and pepper into your Instant Pot.
2. Press the SLOW COOK button, adjust the temperature to LOW, and adjust the time to 8 hours.
3. Make sure the steam valve is set to "vent".
4. After 8 hours, remove the lid and use a hand-held blender to whizz the until the soup is very smooth.
5. Add salt, pepper, and the coconut cream, stir through, and serve!

Loaded Veggie Stew with Mash (V, VG)

Stew and mashed potatoes is like your favorite jumper, it's not very glamorous, but it's so comforting. This stew is loaded with veggies, and served on a creamy potato mash.

Time: approximately 30 minutes

Ingredients:
- Olive oil
- 1 onions, roughly chopped
- 4 garlic cloves, finely chopped
- 4fl oz red wine
- 2 large carrots, peeled and chopped into chunks
- 4 Portobello mushrooms, sliced
- 2 parsnips, peeled and chopped into chunks
- 1 medium-sized sweet potato, chopped into chunks
- 2 zucchinis, chopped into chunks
- 1 tin tomatoes
- 16fl oz vegetable stock
- 1 sprig fresh rosemary
- Salt and pepper, to taste
- 16 oz potatoes, peeled and chopped into chunks
- 4fl oz coconut cream

Method:
1. Drizzle some olive oil into your Instant Pot and press the SAUTE button, keep the temperature at NORMAL.
2. Add the onions, garlic, and red wine to the hot pot, sauté for about 5 minutes until the onions are soft and the alcohol has evaporated from the wine.
3. Add the carrots, mushrooms, parsnips, sweet potato, zucchinis, tinned tomatoes, stock, rosemary, salt, and pepper, stir to combine.
4. Secure the lid onto the pot and press the MEAT/STEW button, adjust the time to 20 minutes.
5. As the stew cooks, boil or steam your potatoes using whichever method you find works best (I simply boil mine in salted water then drain), add the coconut cream, salt, and pepper and mash with a potato masher until you reach the desired consistency – I like mine with a few lumps!
6. Once the pot beeps, quick-release the pressure and remove the lid, stir the stew.
7. Serve the stew on top of a pile of creamy mash.

Creamy Spinach Polenta and Fried Mushrooms (V)

Portobello mushrooms, soaked in egg and breadcrumbs, fried in olive oil. A bed of creamy polenta, speckled with emerald spinach.

Time: approximately 25 minutes

Ingredients:
- Olive oil
- 4 large Portobello mushrooms
- 1 egg, lightly beaten
- ½ cup breadcrumbs
- 16fl oz vegetable stock
- 4fl oz cream
- Salt and pepper, to taste
- 1 cup (about 6 oz) instant polenta
- 1 tbsp butter
- 1 cup baby spinach leaves, roughly chopped

Method:
1. Drizzle some olive oil into your Instant Pot and press the SAUTE button, keep the temperature at NORMAL.
2. Dip the mushrooms into the beaten egg and then dip them straight into the breadcrumbs until full coated (use more breadcrumbs if needed).
3. Place the crumbed mushrooms into the hot pot and fry on both sides until golden and crispy, about 7 minutes in total.
4. Remove the mushrooms from the pot and set aside as you prepare the polenta, no need to wash the pot.
5. Add the vegetable stock, cream, salt, and pepper to the pot and bring to a simmer.
6. Add the polenta and spinach to the pot as you whisk continuously, keep whisking as the polenta becomes thick and creamy.
7. Add the butter to the polenta and allow it to melt before whisking to combine.
8. Serve the mushrooms on top of a bed of creamy polenta!

Breakfast

If you're the kind of person who neglects breakfast...then you'd better change your tune, because the Instant Pot can make some of the tastiest breakfasts around. These recipes are a mixture of healthy and not-so-healthy options for weekdays and weekends.

Vanilla Date Oatmeal

Oatmeal gives you the energy to ace the day's activities. This recipe uses the warming flavor of vanilla, and the caramel-like quality of dates.

Time: approximately 20 minutes

Ingredients:
- 1 ¾ cups rolled oats (I use whole oats but you can use any you have)
- 24fl oz milk (or 12floz water and 12floz milk)
- 2 tsp vanilla extract
- 8 dates, chopped into small pieces
- Pinch of salt

Method:
1. Place the oats, milk (and water if using), vanilla, dates, and a good pinch of salt into your Instant Pot, stir to combine.
2. Secure the lid onto the pot and press the MANUAL button, cook on LOW pressure for 15 minutes.
3. Once the pot beeps, quick-release the pressure and remove the lid, stir the oatmeal.
4. Serve with sliced bananas and a drizzle of maple syrup, or fresh berries and a dollop of yogurt (it's all up to you, great creative).

Mango Banana Pancakes

Mango again! I was feeling mango-deprived so I had to sneak it into another recipe. These tropical-inspired pancakes are actually pretty healthy if you don't add extra sugars or fats, so you can eat them all week long. I top mine with plain yoghurt and a spoonful of LSA.

Time: approximately 20 minutes

Ingredients:
- Coconut oil
- 1 ¼ cups plain flour
- 1 tsp baking powder
- 2 bananas, mashed
- 1 ripe mango, peeled, flesh cut into small chunks
- 1 egg, lightly beaten
- 6fl oz coconut milk

Method:
1. Drizzle some coconut oil into your Instant Pot and press the SAUTE button, keep the temperature at NORMAL, prepare the batter as the pot heats up.
2. Sift the flour and baking powder into a bowl.
3. Stir together the mashed bananas, mango pieces, egg, and coconut milk in a small bowl.
4. Add the wet ingredients to the flour and baking powder, gently stir until just combined, don't over mix.
5. Drop large spoonsful of mixture into the hot pot and cook until bubbles appear, flip the pancakes over and cook the other side until golden.
6. Stack them up, top them with fresh fruit and yoghurt, and enjoy!

Pastry-Free Bacon, Egg, and Goat Cheese Tarts

Goat cheese can be found in most supermarkets. It has a unique, creamy flavor and goes very well with bacon and eggs. These tarts can be frozen in advance, to have on hand as a quick and easy breakfast.

Time: approximately 15 minutes

Ingredients:

- 3 eggs, lightly beaten
- 4 bacon rashers, chopped into small pieces
- 2 oz goat cheese, crumbled into small pieces
- Salt and pepper, to taste
- 8 cupcake cases

Method:

1. With a fork, stir together the eggs, bacon pieces, goat cheese, pepper, and salt (only use a tiny pinch of salt as bacon and goat cheese are quite salty).
2. Pour 2 cups of water into the Instant Pot and place a rack into the pot (above the water).
3. Pour the egg mixture into 8 cupcake cases and very carefully place them onto the rack in the pot.
4. Secure the lid onto the pot and press the STEAM button, keep the time at the default 10 minutes.
5. Once the pot beeps, quick-release the pressure and remove the lid.
6. Carefully remove the tarts from the pot and leave them to cool before eating.
7. Freeze leftover tarts in an airtight container in the freezer for up to 3 months.

Peanut Butter and Apricot Breakfast Muffins

These muffins are great for breakfast, but I think they're just as good, if not better for morning tea.

Time: approximately 15 minutes

Ingredients:
- ½ cup peanut butter (any kind)
- 2 tbsp honey
- 6fl oz milk
- 2 eggs, lightly beaten
- 1 ½ cups plain flour
- 1 tsp baking powder
- 12 dried apricots, chopped into small pieces
- 8-12 cupcake cases

Method:
1. Place the peanut butter and honey in a microwave-safe bowl, then into the microwave and heat for about 20 seconds to make it a bit easier to stir.
2. Add the milk and eggs to the peanut butter and honey and whisk until combined and smooth.
3. Sift the flour and baking powder into a large bowl and add the wet ingredients, stir very gently until just combined, don't over mix, don't worry if it looks a bit lumpy!
4. Pour 2 cups of water into the Instant Pot and place a rack into the pot (above the water).
5. Pour the muffin mixture and apricot pieces into 8-12 cupcake cases (depending on the size of your cases, don't fill more than three quarters) and very carefully place them onto the rack in the pot.
6. Secure the lid onto the pot and press the STEAM button, keep the time at the default 10 minutes.
7. Once the pot beeps, quick-release the pressure and remove the lid.
8. Carefully remove the muffins from the pot and leave them to cool before eating.

Slow-Cooked Hot Granola

Oats, seeds, nuts, dried fruits, spices, and apple juice – heated overnight to result in a hot, filling, and nourishing Winter breakfast.

Time: approximately 8 hours

Ingredients:
- 1 ½ cups oats (any kind)
- 2 tbsp pumpkin seeds
- 1 tbsp sunflower seeds
- 1 tbsp whole linseeds
- 20 almonds, chopped
- 10 walnuts, chopped
- 10 pecans, chopped
- 12 dried apricots, chopped
- 10 dates, chopped
- Small handful of dried cranberries
- 1 tsp cinnamon
- 16fl oz pure apple juice
- 8fl oz milk
- Pinch of salt

Method:
1. Place all ingredients, (yup, all of them), plus a very small pinch of salt into your Instant Pot, stir to combine.
2. Secure the lid onto the pot and press the SLOW COOK button, adjust the temperature to LOW and set the time to 8 hours.
3. Make sure the steam valve is set to "vent".
4. Once the pot beeps, quick-release the steam and remove the lid.
5. Stir the granola, if it's too thick for your liking you can add a bit more milk or apple juice.
6. Serve with cold milk or yoghurt.

"Fancy" Scrambled Eggs with Smoked Fish

These scramble eggs are "fancy" because they include smoked fish, cream, and a shaving of parmesan cheese. These are the kind of eggs you make when you're trying to impress!

Time: approximately 10 minutes

Ingredients:
- 4 eggs, lightly beaten
- 3 tbsp cream
- Salt and pepper, to taste
- 2 oz smoked fish (any kind, but salmon is perfect), flaked
- 1 tbsp butter
- Parmesan cheese (to serve, only a small amount needed)

Method:
1. With a fork, stir together the eggs, cream, salt, and pepper, add the smoked fish and gently stir it through.
2. Add the butter to the Instant Pot and press the SAUTE button, adjust the temperature to LOW.
3. Once the butter has melted, add the egg mixture to the pot and gently push the sides of the eggs with a spatula as they slowly cook.
4. Once the eggs have just cooked but are still slightly runny and glossy, transfer them to bowls and grate a small amount of Parmesan cheese over each serving.
5. Serve with toast and coffee!

Breakfast Bars

I love these breakfast bars because they remind me of cake...but without the unhealthy ingredients. Banana, berries, and coconut are the main flavors in these tasty bars. You will need a small sheet pan which fits inside your Instant Pot.

Time: approximately 30 minutes

Ingredients:
- 2 bananas, mashed
- 1 tsp vanilla extract
- 2 eggs, lightly beaten
- 1 tsp baking powder
- ½ cup whole meal flour
- ½ cup desiccated coconut
- 1 cup frozen berries (any kind, I use raspberries)
- ½ cup chopped walnuts
- 1 cup ground almonds

Method:
1. Prepare your sheet pan by lining it with baking paper (ensure it fits in your Instant Pot).
2. Stir together the bananas, vanilla, and eggs.
3. Sift the baking powder and flour into a large bowl and add the coconut, stir to combine.
4. Add the banana mixture to the flour and gently stir.
5. Add the berries, walnuts, and almonds and gently fold them into the mixture.
6. Pour the mixture into your prepared pan.
7. Pour 2 cups of water into the Instant Pot and place a rack into the pot (above the water).
8. Place the pan onto the rack and press the MANUAL button, cook on LOW for 25 minutes.
9. Once the pot beeps, quick-release the pressure and remove the lid.
10. Remove the pan and leave on a board or heat-proof surface to cook before turning out the bars and slicing.
11. Keep the bars in an airtight container in the pantry, or freeze them for up to 3 months.

Creamy Red Wine Mushrooms on Toast

Wine for breakfast? Yup! Mushrooms with red wine, garlic, and cream, poured onto buttered toast. Serve this to your friend or partner and they'll love you forever.

Time: approximately 20 minutes

Ingredients:
- Olive oil
- 4 garlic cloves, finely chopped
- 4fl oz red wine
- 2 cups chopped mushrooms, (any kind, but I use small brown mushrooms)
- 6fl oz cream
- ½ tsp dried mixed herbs
- Salt and pepper, to taste
- 4 slices of sourdough bread
- Butter (for the toast)

Method:
1. Drizzle some olive oil into your Instant Pot and press the SAUTE button, keep the temperature at NORMAL.
2. Add the garlic and wine to the pot and simmer for a few minutes until the alcohol has evaporated from the wine.
3. Add the mushrooms, cream, herbs, salt, and pepper to the pot, stir to combine.
4. Secure the lid onto the pot and press the MANUAL button, cook on HIGH pressure for 8 minutes.
5. Get the toast ready as the mushrooms cook.
6. Once the pot beeps, quick-release the pressure and remove the lid, stir the mushrooms.
7. Serve the mushrooms on buttered toast!

Berry and Chia seed Oatmeal

More oatmeal! This version is not slow cooked, but cooked quickly under high pressure. Chia seeds are available from most supermarkets, and they are absolutely full of fiber and other goodies. Use any berries you like, but I always use raspberries because they're my absolute favorite.

Time: approximately 15 minutes

Ingredients:
- 1 ½ cups oats (any kind, I use whole oats but you can use instant)
- 12 oz water
- 12 oz milk
- 1 cup berries (frozen or fresh)
- 2 tbsp chia seeds
- 1tsp cinnamon
- Pinch of salt

Method:
1. Place the oats, water, milk, berries, chia seeds, cinnamon, and a pinch of salt into your Instant Pot and stir to combine.
2. Secure the lid onto the pot and press the MANUAL button, cook on HIGH pressure for 10 minutes.
3. Once the pot beeps, quick-release the pressure and remove the lid.
4. Chia seeds soak-up lots of moisture and become quite gelatinous, so the oatmeal will be very thick.
5. Serve with milk and extra berries.

Slow-Cooked Breakfast Beans

Beans on toast has got to be the most energizing, filling and empowering hot breakfast I can think of. Got a big day ahead with lots of work and maybe a gym session? Start with beans on toast. Cooked overnight for 8 hours, you'll be running to the kitchen as soon as you awake! This recipe makes enough for breakfast for 2, for 2 days (4 servings in total).

Time: approximately 8 hours

Ingredients:
- 1 onion, finely chopped
- 4 garlic cloves, finely chopped
- 2 tins kidney beans, drained
- 1 tin black beans, drained
- 1 tin chopped tomatoes
- 1 tbsp balsamic vinegar
- 1 tbsp brown sugar
- 1 tsp ground paprika
- 1 tsp ground cumin
- 1 tsp ground coriander
- Salt and pepper, to taste

Method:
1. Add all ingredients into the Instant Pot, as well as 1 cup of water and a pinch of salt and pepper, stir to combine.
2. Secure the lid onto the pot and press the SLOW COOK button, adjust the temperature to LOW, and adjust the time to 8 hours.
3. Make sure the steam valve is set to "vent".
4. Once the pot beeps, quick-release the steam, remove the lid, and stir the beans
5. Serve on buttered toast.
6. Keep leftover beans in a covered bowl or container in the fridge for up to 3 days, or freeze in a plastic container for up to 3 months.

Choc-Banana Stuffed French Toast

This is one for special weekends (or holidays!). Dark chocolate and bananas fill egg-coated brioche, and fried to melted perfection. If you want to really go to town with this, then serve with whipped cream and fresh berries. It involves eggs, bread, and it's called "toast", so it is breakfast even though it tastes like dessert.

Time: approximately 25 minutes

Ingredients:
- Butter or coconut oil for frying
- 4 thick slices of brioche (or good-quality white bread)
- 1 banana, sliced
- 3 oz dark chocolate, chopped into small pieces
- 2 eggs, lightly beaten
- 2 tbsp sugar mixed with 1tsp cinnamon and sprinkled on a plate ready for dipping
- 2 tbsp cream

Method:
1. Drizzle the coconut oil or butter into your Instant Pot and press the SAUTE button, keep the temperature at NORMAL.
2. Make two sandwiches by spreading a layer of banana slices onto two pieces of bread, then sprinkle a layer of chopped chocolate over the bananas, then place the other piece of bread on top.
3. Here's where it gets a little bit tricky: have your bowl of beaten eggs ready, carefully pick up each sandwich and dip both sides of it (edges included) into the egg, without spilling the fillings.
4. Transfer the egg-soaked sandwiches to the sugar and cinnamon mixture and coat both sides.
5. Transfer the egg and sugar-coated sandwiches to the hot pot and fry on both sides for about 4 minutes each, or until golden on the outside, and melted and gooey in the middle.
6. Serve with fresh fruits and cream or yogurt!

Stone Fruit, Yogurt, and Toasted Oat Parfait

If you've got an abundance of stone fruits, then make a batch of stewed fruits to layer with yogurt and toasted oats. This parfait is refreshing, filling, sweet, and crunchy.

Time: approximately 35 minutes

Ingredients:
- 2 apricots, stones removed, flesh cut into chunks
- 2 nectarines, stones removed, flesh cut into chunks
- 2 peaches, stones removed, flesh cut into chunks
- 1 tbsp sugar
- 1 tsp vanilla extract
- ½ cup oats
- 1 tbsp honey
- ½ tsp cinnamon
- 1 cup (8fl oz) Greek yogurt, (divided into two, half a cup per serving)

Method:
1. Place all of the fruit into your Instant Pot and add the sugar, vanilla, and 16fl oz of water, stir to combine.
2. Secure the lid onto the pot and press the MEAT/STEW button and adjust the time to 20 minutes.
3. While the fruit cooks, prepare the oats by placing them into a small frying pan over a medium heat, once they begin to turn golden, add the honey and cinnamon, stir to combine, continue to cook for a further 5 minutes or until the oats become golden and the honey melts, take off the heat and set aside.
4. Once the pot beeps, quick-release the pressure and remove the lid, stir the fruit and leave to cool slightly.
5. Place a dollop of stewed fruit into a sundae glass (or bowl), then add a dollop of yoghurt, then sprinkle with the toasted oats, repeat again until you have 2 layers of everything.

Appetizers

These recipes can be made as snacks, appetizers, or tapas for romantic dinners or movie nights. Perfect for picking, snacking, nibbling, and grazing.

Crumbed Chorizo Bites

Chorizo sausage, wrapped in spinach, rolled in breadcrumbs, and cooked in butter and honey – it may sound odd, but they're so yummy! Salty, sweet, spicy. I like to serve with a simple dipping sauce of Greek yoghurt, olive oil, and lemon zest. This recipe makes enough for 2 people...and more for later!

Time: approximately 20 minutes

Ingredients:
- 2 tbsp honey
- 1 tbsp butter
- 2 chorizo sausages (about 4-5 inches long each), cut into even chunks
- 1 egg, lightly beaten
- Small handful of baby spinach leaves
- ½ cup breadcrumbs
- Toothpicks

Method:
1. Place the honey and butter into the Instant Pot, press the SAUTE button, and keep the temperature at NORMAL.
2. Lightly coat the chorizo chunks in beaten egg and wipe off any excess, they need to be just sticky enough to hold onto the spinach.
3. Wrap each chorizo chunk with a spinach leaf.
4. Coat the spinach-wrapped chorizo chunks with another thin layer of egg.
5. Roll the chunks in the breadcrumbs until fully coated.
6. Place a toothpick through the center of each chunk to keep the spinach from falling off as they cook.
7. Add the crumbed chorizo chunks to the hot pot and turn them as they cook.
8. Once they are golden and crispy, they are done!
9. Serve with a cooling dipping sauce of your choice.

Asparagus, Bacon, and Camembert Wraps

I'm really into wrapping things at the moment! Asparagus is paired with camembert, and wrapped in bacon. Place them in your hot Instant Pot and listen to that glorious sizzle! A great appetizer of fancy snack.

Time: approximately 18 minutes

Ingredients:
- Olive oil
- 6 spears of asparagus
- ½ wheel of camembert (about 2.5 oz) cut into 12 small pieces
- 6 bacon rashers

Method:
1. Drizzle some olive oil into the Instant Pot, press the SAUTE button, and keep the temperature at NORMAL.
2. Add the asparagus to the pot and sauté for about 5 minutes or until just starting to soften but not totally cooked through.
3. Remove the asparagus and place onto a board.
4. Press 2 pieces of camembert into each spear of asparagus, it's okay if you slightly mush it, it will stick that way!
5. Tightly wrap each spear of asparagus and camembert with one bacon rasher.
6. Place into the hot pot (the SAUTE function should still be on) and sauté for about 6 minutes, turning once, until the bacon is crispy and the cheese is just starting to melt through.
7. Serve immediately!

Carrot and Pumpkin Hummus Dip

The orange hue of carrot and pumpkin makes this hummus really stand out! It's not just pretty, it's delicious too. Place a bowl of this on the coffee table, with a big bowl of pita bread crisps, rice crackers, or fresh veggie sticks – movie night snack!

Time: approximately 15 minutes

Ingredients:
- 1 large carrot, peeled and chopped into chunks
- 6 oz pumpkin, skin removed, flesh cut into chunks
- Pinch of salt
- 1 tin chickpeas, drained
- 1 tbsp tahini
- 1 garlic clove
- 1 lemon
- Salt and pepper, to taste

Method:
1. Pour 2 cups of water into your Instant Pot and place the steaming basket into the pot.
2. Place the carrot and pumpkin into the basket and sprinkle with salt.
3. Secure the lid onto the pot and press the STEAM button, and keep the time to 10 minutes.
4. Once the pot beeps, quick-release the steam and remove the lid.
5. Place the cooked veggies into a blender or food processor and add the chickpeas, tahini, garlic, juice of one lemon, salt, pepper, and a very generous drizzle of olive oil (about ¼ cup).
6. Blitz until very smooth.
7. Transfer to a bowl and eat with any "dippers" you like!

Walnut, Apple, and Cheese Tarts

These tarts are not just any old snack, they are sophisticated and pretty little bites of crunchiness, saltiness, and sweetness! If you don't like blue cheese? Well, you might be best to skip this one. You will need a small muffin tin to fit into the Instant Pot, or 6 small individual tart tins if you happen to have them. If you can't find a suitable tin, just use a large tart tin and cut the tart into slices once cooked.

Time: approximately 25 minutes

Ingredients:
- 1 tbsp butter, melted (to grease the tins)
- Store bought puff pastry (enough for 6 small tarts)
- 1.5 oz blue cheese, crumbled
- 2 oz ricotta cheese
- 1 egg, lightly beaten
- Pinch of salt
- 1 crisp apple, core removed, flesh cut into thin slices
- 2 tbsp honey
- 8 walnuts, roughly chopped

Method:
1. Pour 1 cup of water into your Instant Pot, place a rack into the pot, and press the MANUAL button, adjust the pressure to LOW, and adjust the time to 15 minutes.
2. Grease your tart tins with butter and line them with puff pastry.
3. In a small bowl, stir together the blue cheese, ricotta cheese, egg, saltuntil combined.
4. Spoon the cheese mixture into the pastry-line tart tins.
5. Cover the top of each filled tart with apple slices (about 2 or 3 slices per tart).
6. Drizzle the tarts with honey (this helps the walnuts to stick to the apple).
7. Sprinkle the tarts with the chopped walnuts.
8. Place the tarts into the Instant Pot and secure the lid.
9. Once the pot beeps, quick-release the pressure and remove the lid, carefully remove the tarts and place them on a board to cool.
10. If you like, you can use a kitchen-grade blow torch to torch the tops of the tarts to create a caramelized effect.

Movie Night Sweet and Salty Snacks

These snacks are so decadent, so only make them if you're fully prepared to enjoy them without any guilt! (No need for food-related guilt anyway, everyone's allowed a treat in my opinion). This batch makes more than enough for 2 people for 2 movie nights. You could finish-off the whole batch in one sitting but I will warn you... there's a LOT of chocolate in there.

Time: approximately 1 hour and 30 minutes including cooling time

Ingredients:
- 1 cup mixed nuts (walnuts, pecans, and cashews are great, but use any and all!)
- ¼ cup pumpkin seeds
- Pinch of salt
- 1 tbsp sunflower oil
- 1 cup pretzels
- 1 cup corn flakes (yes, trust me)
- ½ cup banana chips
- ½ cup milk chocolate chips
- ½ cup white chocolate chips
- ½ cup dark chocolate chips (you can halve the chocolate quantities if it's too much for you)
- 1 tsp sea salt

Method:
1. Press the SAUTE button on your Instant Pot and keep the temperature at NORMAL.
2. Add the nuts and seeds to the hot pot and add a pinch of the sea salt.
3. Stir as the nuts and seeds gently toast.
4. Add the sunflower oil and stir to combine.
5. Add the pretzels, corn flakes, banana chips, all chocolate, and sea salt.
6. Stir as the ingredients slowly start to melt together and the chocolate begins to bind the ingredients.
7. Once most of the chocolate has melted but not completely (still some intact chocolate chips remaining), tip the mixture out onto a lined baking sheet and place into the fridge for about an hour, or until set.
8. Break the cooled and set snacks into bite size pieces and place them in a bowl for immediate nibbling, or keep them in the fridge in an airtight container until you need them.

Cream of Mushroom Soup for Two

Soup as an appetizer is such an elegant and classy way to begin a lovely meal. This cream of mushroom soup has subtle flavors of thyme and garlic.

Time: approximately 25 minutes

Ingredients:

- 2 cups chopped mushrooms, (use any mushrooms you like, I like to use a mixture)
- 1 potato, peeled and chopped into chunks (adds thickness to the soup)
- 4 garlic cloves, finely chopped
- 1 tsp dried rosemary
- 16fl oz vegetable or chicken stock
- Salt and pepper, to taste
- 6fl oz cream

Method:

1. Place the mushrooms, potato, garlic, rosemary, stock, salt, and pepper into your Instant Pot, stir to combine.
2. Secure the lid onto the pot and press the SOUP button, adjust the time to 20 minutes.
3. Once the pot beeps, quick-release the pressure and remove the lid.
4. With a hand-held stick blender, whizz the soup until smooth.
5. Stir the cream into the soup and add another pinch of salt and pepper to taste.
6. Serve with a dainty drizzle of cream on top!

Layered Bean, Cheese, and Spinach Hot Dip

This is quite a comprehensive dip indeed – it has layers of beans, spinach and cheese.
You will need a small, heat-proof bowl for this recipe.

Time: approximately 20 minutes

Ingredients:
- 1 tin cannellini beans, drained (about 1 ½ cups)
- ½ tin red kidney beans, drained (about 3/4 cup)
- 2 garlic cloves, finely chopped
- Salt and pepper, to taste
- 1 cup baby spinach leaves, roughly chopped
- 7 oz ricotta cheese
- 2.5 oz grated cheddar cheese

Method:
1. Place cannellini beans, kidney beans, garlic, salt, and pepper in a small bowl and mash with a hand-held stick blender until smooth.
2. Place 1/3 of the bean mixture into the bottom of a small heat-proof bowl.
3. Add a layer of chopped spinach.
4. Add a layer of ricotta cheese, then sprinkle with cheddar.
5. Repeat until there are 3 layers each of beans, spinach, ricotta, and cheddar.
6. Cover the bowl with baking paper and tie it around the bowl with string to secure.
7. Pour 1 cup of water into your Instant Pot and place a rack into the pot (above the water).
8. Place the bowl onto the rack, secure the lid onto the pot, press the MANUAL button and cook at HIGH pressure for 10 minutes.
9. Once the pot beeps, quick-release the pressure, remove the lid, and carefully take the bowl of dip out of the pot and set it on a board to cool slightly before serving.
10. Serve with crusty bread or veggie sticks for dipping!

Capsicum, Tomato, Basil, and Mozzarella Bruschetta

Bruschetta usually uses fresh tomatoes, but this recipe changes it up a bit and uses cooked tomatoes which have been pressure-cooked until rich and thick. While this is a perfect idea for a starter, it's also a lovely and light main meal too.

Time: approximately 25 minutes

Ingredients:
- 2 large tomatoes, chopped into small pieces
- 1 red capsicum, core and seeds removed, flesh cut into slices
- 1 onion, finely chopped
- 4 garlic cloves, finely chopped
- 1 tsp sugar
- 1 tsp vinegar (red wine vinegar would be ideal)
- Salt and pepper, to taste
- 4 slices of French baguette, brushed with olive oil and sprinkled with salt
- 2 oz mozzarella, grated or cut into chunks (depending on what kind of mozzarella you have, fresh mozzarella can be shredded into chunks)
- Fresh basil

Method:
1. Place the tomatoes, capsicum, onion, garlic, sugar, vinegar, salt, pepper, and 4oz of water into your Instant Pot, stir to combine.
2. Secure the lid onto the pot, press the MANUAL button, and cook on HIGH pressure for 8 minutes.
3. As the veggies are cooking, toast your baguette slices in the oven under the grill until golden.
4. Once the pot beeps, quick-release the pressure and remove the lid.
5. Spread a generous amount of tomato mixture onto the toasted bread slices, top with mozzarella cheese, then place 2 basil leaves on each one.
6. Drizzle with olive oil to finish!

Honey-Glazed Meatballs

These meatballs are made from minced pork and are doused in a sticky honey glaze. Make a quick batch of these to snack on with your partner as you cook your main course.

Time: approximately 15 minutes

Ingredients:
- 10 oz minced pork
- 2 garlic cloves, finely chopped
- ½ tsp ground ginger
- 1 egg, lightly beaten
- 1/3 cup breadcrumbs
- Salt and pepper, to taste
- Olive oil
- 3 tbsp honey
- 2 tbsp soy sauce
- 1 tsp sesame oil

Method:
1. Combine the minced pork, garlic, ginger, egg, breadcrumbs, salt, and pepper in a bowl and roll the mixture into balls.
2. Drizzle some olive oil into your Instant Pot and press the SAUTE button, keep the temperature at NORMAL.
3. Add the meatballs to the hot pot and cook for about 5 minutes, turning a few times, until they are golden brown.
4. Add the honey, soy sauce, and sesame oil to the pot and gently stir into the meatballs (without breaking or crumbling them).
5. Sauté for another 5 minutes until the meatballs are cooked through and the glaze is sticky.
6. Serve with tooth picks.

Mini Corn Fritters with Salsa

Corn fritters are even yummier when they're in mini form! (Don't ask how...they just are). These fritters are topped with fresh tomato salsa and sea salt.

Time: approximately 15 minutes

Ingredients:
- Olive oil
- 1 tin corn kernels, drained (about 1 ½ cups)
- 1 egg, lightly beaten
- ½ cup plain flour
- ½ tsp ground cumin
- 2 fresh tomatoes, chopped into small pieces
- Small handful of fresh parsley, finely chopped

Method:
1. Drizzle some olive oil into your Instant Pot, press the SAUTE button, and keep the temperature at NORMAL.
2. Combine the corn kernels and egg in a bowl, whisk the flour and cumin into the bowl with a pinch of salt and pepper and stir to combine.
3. Drop small spoonsful of mixture into the hot pot and cook for about 2 minutes, flip over and cook the other side until both sides are golden.
4. Repeat until all the mixture is used.
5. Place the cooked fritters on a plate and top with the chopped fresh tomatoes, chopped parsley, a drizzle of olive oil, and a pinch of salt.

Chili Wings

This one's for all the chili lovers out there! Chicken wings, sprinkled with chili, and cooked to perfection in your Instant Pot. This is the kind of starter you serve when there's a good game (or movie which is more likely in my case) on TV, and you just feel like nibbling on some chicken as you hang out with your favorite person.

Time: approximately 20 minutes

Ingredients:
- 12 oz chicken wings
- 6fl oz chicken stock
- 1 fresh red chili, finely chopped
- 1 tbsp maple syrup (helps the chili to stick to the chicken, and adds a sweet touch)
- Salt and pepper, to taste

Method:
1. Place the chicken wings, stock, chili, maple syrup, salt, and pepper into your Instant Pot and stir thoroughly to combine and coat the chicken.
2. Secure the lid onto the pot and press the POULTRY button, keep the time to the default 15 minutes.
3. Once the pot beeps, quick-release the pressure and remove the lid.
4. Transfer the wings (and the sauce) onto a serving plate, with a side of napkins as your fingers are bound to get pretty messy!

Desserts

The best part! Desserts! The Instant Pot can take you all the way from breakfast to dessert. Sauces, pies, cheesecake and classics such as apple crumble feature in this sweet section.

White and Milk Chocolate Swirl-Covered Strawberries

This recipe is for couples and new romances – what's more romantic and sweet than strawberries and chocolate? The "swirl" is very easy to do, but looks incredibly impressive.

Time: approximately 1 hour including cooling time

Ingredients:
- 3 tbsp cream
- 3 oz white chocolate, broken into pieces
- 3 oz milk chocolate, broken into pieces
- 8 large strawberries, stalks left intact

Method:
1. Place the cream, white chocolate, and milk chocolate into your Instant Pot and press the SAUTE button, adjust the temperature to LOW.
2. Very gently stir as the chocolate melts, to ensure it doesn't catch on the bottom, but don't stir too vigorously as you don't want to mix the two colors.
3. Once all of the chocolate has melted, very gently swirl it with a fork to create a marbled effect.
4. Dip the strawberries into the chocolate to cover them as much as you can (up to the stalk is ideal, the more chocolate the better).
5. Place the strawberries onto a tray lined with baking paper and place into the fridge to set.

Marshmallow, Chocolate, and Peanut Cups

Another playful recipe for a sweet and sticky treat. Barely any cooking required here, just open a few packets, melt some ingredients together, throw it all in the fridge...then nibble away!

Time: approximately 1 hour including cooling time

Ingredients:

- ¼ cup cream
- 1 cup mini marshmallows
- 3.5 oz milk chocolate, broken into pieces
- 2 tbsp butter
- ½ cup salted peanuts
- 6 paper cupcake cases

Method:

1. Place the cream, marshmallows, chocolate, butter, and peanuts into your Instant Pot, secure the lid onto the pot and press the MANUAL button, cook on LOW for 10 minutes.
2. Once the pot beeps, quick-release the pressure and remove the lid.
3. Give the mixture a stir and spoon into the paper cupcake cases.
4. Place the filled cases onto a plate and place into the fridge to set.

Little Apple Crumbles

You will need 2 individual pie tins or heat-proof ramekins for this recipe. Sweet, tart apples topped with sweet and buttery crumble.

Time: approximately 20 minutes

Ingredients:
- 3 tbsp butter, softened
- 2 tbsp brown sugar
- 2 tbsp plain flour
- ½ tsp cinnamon
- 2 Granny Smith apples, core removed, flesh cut into slices

Method:
1. Place the butter, brown sugar, flour, and cinnamon into a small bowl and stir to combine until a rough crumble forms.
2. Place the apple slices into 2 ramekins or pie tins and sprinkle with a little extra brown sugar for added sweetness.
3. Top the apples with the crumble mixture.
4. Pour 1 cup of water into your Instant Pot and place a rack into the pot (above the water).
5. Place the crumbles onto the rack, secure the lid onto the pot, press the MANUAL button, and cook on HIGH pressure for 10 minutes.
6. Once the pot beeps, quick-release the pressure and remove the lid.
7. Carefully remove the crumbles and place them on a board to cool.
8. Serve with vanilla ice cream!

Banana and Caramel Cakes

These little cakes are inspired by upside down cakes - they have a gooey pile of banana and golden syrup at the bottom, which oozes down over the cake once you turn them upside down on your serving plates.

Time: approximately 20 minutes

Ingredients:
- 1 tbsp butter, melted (to grease ramekins)
- 1 egg
- 4fl oz milk
- 2 tbsp butter, melted
- ¾ cup plain flour
- ½ tsp baking powder
- 1 banana, sliced
- 2 tbsp golden syrup

Method:
1. Pour 1 cup of water into your Instant Pot and place a rack into the pot (above the water).
2. Prepare two mini cake tins or heat-proof ramekins by greasing with butter.
3. Whisk together the egg, milk, and butter.
4. Sieve the flour and baking powder into the wet ingredients and gently stir until combined.
5. Lay the banana slices into the bottom of the ramekins and pour the golden syrup over the top (1/2 a banana and 1tbsp syrup per ramekin).
6. Divide the cake mixture between the two ramekins.
7. Place the cake-filled ramekins or tins onto the rack in the Instant Pot, press the MANUAL button, and cook on HIGH for 12 minutes.
8. Once the pot beeps, quick-release the pressure and remove the lid.
9. Carefully place the cakes onto a board to cool.
10. Turn the cakes out (upside down) onto a plate before serving with cream or ice cream.

Lemon Custard

Time: approximately 20 minutes

Ingredients:
- 2 egg yolks
- 1 tsp custard powder
- 8fl oz cream
- 1 tbsp sugar
- 2 lemons

Method:
1. Place the egg yolks, custard powder, cream, sugar, zest and juice of two lemons into a small heat-proof bowl and whisk to combine.
2. Pour 2 cups of water into your Instant Pot and place a rack into the pot (above the water).
3. Place the bowl of custard onto the rack, secure the lid onto the pot, press the MANUAL button, and cook on LOW for 15 minutes.
4. Once the pot beeps, quick-release the pressure and remove the lid.
5. Carefully remove the bowl of custard from the pot and place it onto a board to cool.
6. Serve on its own, with fruit, or with other desserts such as cakes and tarts!

Slow-Cooked Apples in Caramel Sauce

Time: approximately 8 hours

Ingredients:

- 2 apples, core removed, flesh cut into fifths
- ¼ cup brown sugar
- 3 tbsp butter
- 8fl oz cream
- 1 tsp vanilla extract

Method:

1. Place the apples, brown sugar, butter, cream, and vanilla into your Instant Pot and stir to combine.
2. Secure the lid onto the pot and press the SLOW COOK button, adjust the temperature to LOW, and adjust the time to 8 hours.
3. Make sure the steam valve is set to "vent".
4. Once the pot beeps, quick-release the steam and remove the lid.
5. Serve your lovely, soft, caramel-coated apples with vanilla ice cream!

Blackberry, Ginger, and White Chocolate Pies

Blackberries, ginger, and white chocolate in a fluffy ricotta cheese filling, all encased in sweet short crust pastry. This recipe makes 4 one-person pies, so you can each have one now, and have another one stashed away for later.

Time: approximately 20 minutes

Ingredients:
- 1 tbsp butter, melted
- Store-bought sweet short crust pastry (enough to line 4 individual pie tins)
- 1 ½ cups blackberries
- ½ tsp ground ginger
- 3 oz white chocolate, chopped into small pieces
- ½ cup ricotta cheese
- 1 egg
- 1 tbsp sugar

Method:
1. Prepare the pie tins by greasing with butter and lining with store bought sweet short crust pastry.
2. In a small bowl, mix together the blackberries, ginger, white chocolate, ricotta, egg, and sugar until combined.
3. Spoon the blackberry mixture into the pastry-lined pie tins.
4. Pour 2 cups of water into your Instant pot and place a rack into the pot (above the water).
5. Place the pie tins onto the rack and secure the lid onto the pot.
6. Press the MANUAL button and cook at a HIGH pressure for 12 minutes.
7. Once the pot beeps, quick-release the pressure and remove the lid.
8. Carefully remove the pies from the pot and place on a board to cool.
9. Turn the pies out onto your serving plates and serve with vanilla ice cream (of course).

Date-Night Cheesecakes

I call these "date-night cheesecakes" because they're filled with berries and chocolate, both of which I consider to be very romantic foods. However, don't hesitate to make these for any non-romantic friends! They won't get any ideas, I promise.

Time: approximately 35 minutes

Ingredients:
- 1 tbsp butter, melted (to grease the ramekins)
- 2.5 oz plain vanilla or chocolate store-bought biscuits, crushed
- 3 tbsp butter, melted
- 6 oz cream cheese
- 1 egg
- 2 oz sour cream
- 1 tbsp sugar
- ½ cup mixed berries
- 4 oz milk chocolate, chopped into small pieces

Method:
1. Prepare 4 individual ramekins or tart tins by greasing with butter.
2. Mix together the crushed biscuits and melted butter and press into the bottom and up the sides of the ramekins or tins.
3. Whisk together the cream cheese, egg, sour cream, sugar, berries, and chocolate until smooth.
4. Pour the cream cheese mixture into the biscuit-lined tins.
5. Pour 2 cups of water into your Instant Pot and place a rack into the pot (above the water).
6. Place the filled ramekins onto the rack and secure the lid onto the pot.
7. Press the MANUAL button and cook at a HIGH pressure for 15 minutes.
8. Once the pot beeps, allow the pressure to naturally release for about 5 minutes before quick-releasing the rest.
9. Remove the lid, remove the cheesecakes from the pot and place onto a rack to cool.
10. Serve with extra berries and a shaving of chocolate on top!

Coconut, Chocolate, and Cherry Cakes (Cheats Version)

Time: approximately 15 minutes

Ingredients:
- 1 tbsp butter, melted
- 3fl oz cream
- 2 tbsp sugar
- Store-bought sponge cake, enough for 4 ramekins
- 3 tbsp desiccated coconut
- 3 oz dark chocolate
- 15 fresh cherries, stones removed, flesh roughly chopped
- Whipped cream, to serve

Method:
1. Prepare the ramekins by greasing with butter.
2. Stir together the cream and sugar.
3. Press squares of store-bought sponge into each ramekin (doesn't need to be tidy, just press it in tightly).
4. Spoon the cream and sugar mixture over each sponge-lined ramekin.
5. Sprinkle the desiccated coconut over top, then the chocolate, and finally the cherries.
6. Pour 2 cups of water into your Instant Pot and place a rack into the pot (above the water).
7. Place the filled ramekins onto the rack and secure the lid onto the pot.
8. Press the MANUAL button and cook at a HIGH pressure for 10 minutes.
9. Once the pot beeps, quick-release the pressure and remove the lid.
10. Take the ramekins out of the pot and place them onto a board to cool slightly.
11. Top the cakes with whipped cream and extra cherries to serve!

Spiked Double Chocolate Sauce

White chocolate, dark chocolate, and brandy are a power trio! This sauce is good enough to be eaten straight from the spoon, but it's yummiest when drizzled over ice cream.

Time: approximately 15 minutes

Ingredients:
- 3 oz dark chocolate, broken into pieces
- 3 oz milk chocolate, broken into pieces
- 8fl oz cream
- 2fl oz brandy

Method:
1. Place the dark chocolate, milk chocolate, cream, and brandy into your Instant Pot and press the SAUTE button, adjust the temperature to LOW.
2. Stir as the chocolate melts and gently reaches a light simmer.
3. Once all of the chocolate has melted and the sauce is thick and glossy, transfer to a jar or jug.
4. Serve immediately or store in the fridge.
5. Serve over ice cream, and keep out of reach of children!

CONCLUSION

If you're the cook of your household of two, then by now I bet you've completely blown your partner away with your amazing Instant Pot skills!

I hope you've enjoyed these recipes and you've discovered some new flavor combinations to experiment with. Feel free to change and adjust these recipes to suit your tastes, they're here to inspire you!

Remember that cooking for two doesn't need to be restrictive. It doesn't need to put you off making dishes with intricate flavors and textures. And hey, if you end up making too much? Hello leftovers and midnight snacks! It's a win-win cooking situation.

Made in the USA
Lexington, KY
15 January 2018